The Brow of Dawn

The Brow of Dawn

One Woman's Journey with MS

Catherine Edward

B&B
Bunim & Bannigan
New York Charlottetown

Published in the United States by

BUNIM & BANNIGAN, LTD.
PMB 157 111 East 14th Street New York, NY 10003-4103
Box 636 Charlottetown, PE C1A 7L3 Canada

www.bunimandbannigan.com

A Bunim & Bannigan Personal Wellness Book

Manufactured in the United States of America

Design by Jean Carbain
Cover illustration: Mid-Morning Sky (Detail) by Barry Jeeves

Grateful acknowledgment is given to
The Acorn Press for permission to publish
this title in the United States.

LIBRARY OF CONGRESS
CATALOGING-IN-PUBLICATION DATA

Edward, Catherine.

The brow of dawn : one woman's journey with MS
Catherine Edward. — 1st
B&B ed.

p.   cm.

ISBN 978-1-933480-19-0 (trade pbk.)
1. Edward, Catherine—Health. 2. Multiple sclerosis—Patient—Biography.
I. Title.

RC377.E368 2008   362.196'8340092—dc22
[B]

2008002308

ISBN: 978-1-933480-19-0
ISBN-10: 1-933480-19-X

135798642

First B&B edition

In memory of my remarkable father,
and to Jock, who imagined the book in the first place.

Contents

Foreword

The Brow of Dawn. I love this title. It says a lot about what this book is about, what Catherine Edward is about, and perhaps what all of us should be more about. It suggests that each day is for each of us to make of it what we can, despite the adversities that come to us all. This book shows how one person who happens to have multiple sclerosis lives each of her days.

As a physician I often hear people who have difficulty coping with the slings and arrows that affect their lives state that anyone would respond as they do if they had their troubles. Anyone would crumble and slide into dejection and despair if they had such a problem. On the other hand, my patients also understand that attitude and a positive outlook make all the difference in life and in illness. Some do this naturally. Some learn it. But I have been impressed that most come to an understanding of how they must readapt and live their lives despite adversity, and they continue to amaze me and humble me with their strength and their courage. And no one amazes me more than Mary Catherine Edward, the sparkling strong woman from Prince Edward Island who exudes all the charm, enthusiasm, and toughness of Anne of Green Gables, who came from that same beautiful Island.

You have to meet Catherine to understand her approach to life. As you read her diary, and come to know her, you will be charmed by her wit, engaged by her thoughts, delighted by her insights, uplifted by her spirit, and energized by her strength.

When I first met her, she made it very clear that she was a person, but happens to have a disease. As I came to know her I understood her philosophy, which was something like, "I have a disease—but it is not me—I am well!" This is not a denial; it is an affirmation of the person.

As you read this book, you will see that she does not dwell only on her disease. She has a life, a childhood, a family, experiences, hopes, values, and dreams. She happens to have a disease, and she must deal with that, too. Thus, this is not a diary of a disease—it is a story of how to live your life.

We will all meet adversity in this life. The only question is whether we will have the capacity to meet it with spirit and strength. Catherine's example shows us that it is possible, and although each of us must do this in our own way, she teaches us some very important lessons.

MS is not a minor problem for Catherine. It often saps her energy, interrupts her life, and prevents her from doing some things she dearly wants to do. It gives her all the uncertainty and fears that every person with MS feels. She isn't unrealistic about this, but she has decided how she must live her life.

We have a lot to learn from her.

—Jock Murray, OC, MD, FRCPC,MACP

I am on a journey.
There are many travelers.
My husband holds my hand.
Our children hold our hearts.
We missed the well-marked route.
The journey is still in progress.

The Brow of Dawn

I love to stand out on
the brow of dawn.
Creation at its freshest.
No imprint on the day as yet.
It is mine to make.

I would that I will make it smooth
no wrinkle upon the brow of dawn
impressed by me.

And should I falter
and leave a mark, though
there is a chance to smooth it,
sorrow.
I would be full of it.

Then standing towards the
damask of dusk,
I make my peace
so that when morning comes again
I can kiss the brow of dawn
with all my good intention.

1 ❦ A FAST BEGINNING

Snow Wings

S tep out the door. Put on skis. From there we have a choice of trails. We could go straight down the hill and onto the river. It is best to be warmed up for this route, or to be very young and supple. This is a fast beginning. We could take a more gentle beginning, down the back lane to the hollow and onto the Cove Road. Once at the Cove you meet up with anybody who came the river route. There is an advantage to taking the river route, if you are loose enough to do the hill, as the river is an excellent place to practice one's diagonal stride and, so, warm up quickly. Now everybody is on the River Road and heading into the woods. If the snow is fresh and we must cut trails it is good to have everybody on hand. It is heavy work. Like Canada geese in their "V," we take turns cutting trail.

There is a microclimate in the woods. Still and windless, it feels soft and considerably warmer than out in exposed places. When we get to the Daddy Pine we leave jackets behind. Now where to? Up Sugar Maple Run and over to Victor's Road or the Magic Glade. These are both fast runs since they are steep and winding. After several runs of the five of us flying over them, they can be very fast. If necessary, we can simply impose a crash landing when we reach the bottom of the hill and have to make a fast right turn to avoid hitting a tree at the river's edge. For a long, energetic run, one that requires poling only at the top and some fancy footwork to glide all the way to the River Road, we take the Sugar Maple Run from up top, or the Sunbeam Trail, which faces the setting sun all the way from Magic Glade to where it meets Sugar Maple Run, at the very bottom.

There is nothing quite like cross-country skiing. Where before one could only trudge along in boots—the snow heavy against shin and ankle—a switch to skis changes everything. Fly, sail, glide across the snow! Snow wings! A new body that effortlessly wings across field and through woods, cheeks red with sweet cold, and body warm, as warm as summer.

Then, at the end, we must gather up our jackets for the cold ski home, facing the biting wind. Once we leave the hollow and head up the lane toward home, the wind cuts right through every layer. So strong we have to lean into it. It picks on the cheeks and makes eyes water. Push! Push! Up the hill and to the house. Nothing looks so inviting as the house in the distance, light in the windows and smoke rising from the chimney, wending its warm smoke path. It is nearly dark, for we lose all sense of time as our eyes adjust to the failing light. Oh! that wonderful feeling of freezing, well won and soon to end in hearthside comforts. (How I love that.) The clicking sound of skis coming off then plunged into the snow, resting along the side of the house. Click, click. Click, click. Till we all tumble into warmth and supper, for now it is late, we're hungry, and the light is inside.

Again the seasons change, and I move the summer things to the back of the closet and pull out my winter clothes. There are my ski knickers, safe on their hanger. And, once more, I put them forward. How many years has it been since I have worn them? Six, maybe seven? Multiple sclerosis, MS, made it difficult for me to ski. The growing weakness in my right side, especially my leg, left me grounded. Off my snow wings. At first, I held on to the hope I might get better enough to do my favorite winter thing, and later I refused to part with the knickers. Is it possible I will wear them again?

After I lost my balance, I tried and tried, but it was a lost cause. Balance is the very thing needed to ski. I kept my Lifa undershirt and tights until Cecily needed them. I hoarded my long wool ski socks. My mitts disappeared with one of the kids. I keep lots of sweaters. I have my down vest. I could cobble together the gear. Nobody gets the knickers. Mine. I was so pleased to have knickers after skiing in jeans. The snow always stuck to them, and it wasn't very comfortable. But the knickers! Perfectly cut for easy movement. Light, but lined and cozy. Snow can't stick to them. They were a Christmas present from Michael.

Every year I think it is the year for snow wings again. This thought is in the form of a dream.

I wing over the trails in my memory. When spring comes I put the knickers to the back of the closet. In the fall, I pull them forward, with the care of a ritual tradition. I am interested to see how long I will keep this up.

Just Young

There are no memories before Oregon, since I was still a baby when we left New Brunswick. Daddy said it was meant to be an adventure, and, with such an offer, difficult for a young psychiatric doctor to turn down. With two little ones and a few possessions our parents left the salt breeze of the Atlantic and family in Cape Breton and the South Shore of Nova Scotia, for the wheat fields, tumbleweed, and dust storms of eastern Oregon.

It was there I place the first memory of my very own, not one supported by photographs. It is of my brother Tom and me on a hot summer day running through the sprinkler. I was three years old, which made Tom five. A big black car drove up to the house next door. "Next door" is a loose term, for this was a country campus of ten rambling homes for psychiatrists and their families, part of a five-hundred-acre complex which was the State Hospital. A family got out of the car. A little girl just my size, a bigger boy just Tom's size, a father, and a mother with a baby in her arms. Susan and Ralph joined our running-through-the-sprinkler game, and we were immediately bonded. The man and woman turned out to be Uncle Frank and Auntie Pearl, and the baby was Nancy. They came from Canada, too. That is just the way it happened. Sometimes people come into your life as if they had always been there. The place to hold them is kept open till they arrive.

This was the beginning of my memory box, and it filled abundantly from that day on.

Ours was definitely not an ordinary sort of life, and perhaps it was not even reasonable, but it was lots of fun. We had a maid named Marion. She made pink cookies with green icing, did fine tatting and embroidery, and sewed dresses with only a needle and thread, no machine, very clever. I watched her fingers. We had a gardener named Percy, who was also a barber and set up shop in our basement on Saturdays and trimmed the doctors' hair. Percy and Marion called me Kitty. Daddy called me Powerful Katrinka. All the doctors' houses were tended in this way, a maid and a gardener for each. These helpers were patients who were pretty well but not quite yet ready to rejoin the outside world. To us they became family. There were extra gardeners who came once a week to mow the lawns, and there were window washers, electricians, carpenters, painters, plumbers anytime you needed them. Each house had a commissary in the basement, which was kept stocked like a personal grocery store. There was a bakery that delivered fresh bread and baked goods, a butcher to fill any order. "Company coming? Yes, a half-a-dozen porterhouse on the way over." A truck came weekly and took away a big laundry bin on which was printed "Cottage 3"—our house. Marion did the fine washables. There were greenhouses to ensure a constant supply of fresh flowers for in the house because, really, wouldn't it be too grievous to cut flowers blooming in the garden? You could request any color of bouquet. I often wandered about the greenhouses.

The hospital complex included a large, operating farm. As well as providing the food supply for the whole operation, it was an imaginative work program. We children were allowed free range of the farm and so made regular visits to see cows and pigs or hundreds of baby chicks, newly hatched. One evening Tom and Ralph and Susan and I slipped across to the farm against parental orders. It was a misconduct that would have passed unnoticed, had I not fallen into the pig feed. We went home doomed by my misfortune, but they shouldn't have dared me to walk along the pig trough.

The campus was surrounded by hundreds of acres of wheat fields. There were lots of adventures to be had—canyons in those wheat fields, an extraordinary rock formation along the second hill, which provided the site for many make-believe dramas. We had our dear Trixie dog who had a perpetual weight problem due to her regular visits to the baker and the butcher; Taffy the cat and often kittens; two male . . . ahem . . . rabbits, then dozens more; three ducks supposedly for eating, but they became pets and had to be given to people more hard-hearted about these things. Tom and I had turtles we tried to train to race, but that was pretty dull, and I had a goldfish, but one day the bowl was empty, and we noticed a satisfied grin on Taffy's fur face.

The campus provided its particular adventures. Susan and I had rounds, which we made regularly. We'd start at Dr. Gish's. He had a pet alligator that ran away, likely dissatisfied with his quarters, when he, the alligator, was about a foot long. Dr. Gish was also a rock collector. These he stored and sorted and polished in his basement, which consequently had the most black widow spiders in the neighborhood, since spiders liked the rocks as habitat. We were taught to be careful. Mrs. Gish was a leatherworker of exceptional talent, who made intricate designs, usually western, on belts and bags and such. They had two children who were a little odd, and we never really got to know them.

Next, Dr. Silk's. Mrs. Silk stayed in bed every day till eleven reading the *New York Times*, and she seemed to like having us drop by and visit her in her bedroom. Her daughter, Nan, our babysitter, was a high school girl to be worshipped. Nan was a photographer and had her own darkroom. She took pictures of us, and we got to watch her develop them. In the Silks' backyard was a huge brick barbecue with a large smooth steel stovetop. This is where Sue and I practiced our tap dancing. One day I climbed to very nearly the top of a huge birch tree in Nan's front yard. I was so high up I swayed in the breeze up there. Only the birds were up higher. Nan climbed quite a way into the tree to talk me down. There were more birch trees in a small grove between the Silks' and the Calhouns'. That grove was very special to me, because in the spring it was full of purple violets. I would sit there in that fragrant loveliness and imagine it must be what heaven smelled like. My own violet grove.

Dr. Calhoun's was next. Mrs. Calhoun could be depended upon for a treat as long as we were good, polite little girls who listened patiently to stories about grandchildren. We liked that. On Halloween, Dr. Calhoun would gather all us campus trick-or-treaters in and show us a short cowboy movie, or maybe cartoons. This was pretty special in the 1950s.

Next on our rounds was Dr. Weir's. He was the superintendent and lived in the largest house on the top of the hill. There was a rock garden for walking in and an enclosed garden at the back, which we only dared view from the lane as we walked all around the back of the house. It looked like the Secret Garden to us, full of arbors and pagodas and many exotic trees. There was a dear little doghouse, white-shingled with green trim with a small gable over the front door. One day, because the dogs had both died, the house was sent to Tom and me as a gift. It had electricity. The interior was entirely of tongue-and-groove paneling, with an oriental carpet on the floor and miniature, dog-sized twin beds (one for each dog). There was a corner table and some shelves. When the girls used it, it was a dollhouse or a pet hospital, but when the boys took over, it was a fort with their rattlesnake rattlers in residence; these they had collected and stored in bottles. Their cap guns and Davy Crockett hats replaced our dishes and teapot. It was an agreeable arrangement but required constant redecorating.

Mrs. Kestler came next. She and Dr. Kestler were older, and she had a magical foreign accent. She made cookies with cardamom in them, for which we had an insatiable appetite that was never completely satisfied because we were always too shy to ask for more, and so we never got enough of them.

When we got to the Stewarts' we would stop and play a little with Briony and Gail. We sort of envied them because they were so spoiled and allowed to get away with things for which we surely would have been banished to our rooms. Dr. and Mrs. Stewart were from England, and we thought they were the most indulgent parents we had ever met. Mrs. Stewart had a particular interest in geography and took it upon herself, one summer, to teach us girls the location of all the countries in the world, together with their capitals, using a large globe as her guide. The Stewarts' household held a peculiar fascination for us. But we never grew close to the girls. Briony had a tantrum one day at our place and hit Tom over the head with the rake, making three holes in his head. You cannot grow close to a girl who makes holes in the head of your only brother.

The last house belonged to Dr. Kennedy. The Kennedys had four rather grown-up children. They were all in junior or senior high school, so only to be admired from a distance. Mrs. Kennedy was very artistic and always had a project on the go. She loved nothing better than to involve two willing girls, like Sue and me, in her latest project. We thought it very neat that their dining room table was always covered with paper, paint, paint brushes, glue, felt, wax, pipe cleaners, crayons, books, dried flowers, cones, and rocks. Our dining room tables were always ready to set for dinner.

One time, on the way home after rounds, we watched some snake eggs hatch—millions of them—and we did not tell Tom and Ralph.

Off campus, our dearest friends were the Gehlings—Auntie Mary and Uncle Vic. (The West treats you like that, brings you in as family. The whole world should be like this.) Uncle Vic was a physician, too, but a radiologist. Catherine Anne and Guy were about the same ages as Tom and me. Others were ever on the way, five in all, as Mary Theresa, Victor, and Anne Marie were added to the family. Auntie Mary always had an especially perky smile on her face when she was pregnant, which was most of the time as far as I could see. One day I heard her tell my mum, "Every time Vic folds his pants over the footstool in our bedroom I get pregnant." It seemed to me the logical solution was to ask Uncle Vic to hang his pants up in the closet, but nobody ever listens to a little kid on these matters.

My godfather, Paul Metivier, was also a psychiatrist, and he was also enticed to the west from the east. He and Daddy were best friends, and they usually spoke French when they were together, for instance while playing chess. I liked to sit up to the chess table on a small stool and line up the chessmen as they departed the board. This speaking French seemed like a good thing to be able to do, and maybe one day I would have a chance to learn. We didn't speak French because Mother didn't understand a word of it. Besides, who speaks French in Oregon?

At our house the deal was that anyone was welcome, anytime. My mother had an abundant gift of hospitality to indulge on whomever needed it. There was time, too, for with all the help, one could coddle these gifts. She had lots of energy for Parents' (read "mothers'") Committees at school—music, sports, fun days, a hot lunch program. And she and Auntie Pearl carted Sue and me off to dance classes—tap and ballet, also baton and tumbling. There were costumes to make and the eternal battle to try to force my hair into curls, a lost cause. Sue had naturally curly hair. She also had a great advantage in kindergarten with her name. For a time, the task was to print our names before recess. Sue printed "S-u-e" and was off to the swings, while I labored over "M-a-r-y C-a-t-h-e-r-i-n-e." At this point in my life I thought "Jo" would make a perfectly lovely name.

Meanwhile, Mother and Auntie Pearl spent a great deal of time chuckling and laughing over our antics. I supposed they found us highly amusing.

Then, after nearly six years, the call came from New Brunswick. Daddy was needed. His people were calling. The morning came that we went to our last mass at St. Mary's, then back to Auntie Mary and Uncle Vic's for a big Oregon breakfast. And so it was we headed east, the sound of the sea in Daddy's heart. I think we were just outside Walla Walla, Washington, when I asked, "How much farther?" Since it appeared the drive was going to take eleven more days, I did not ask again. Trixie farted all the way through the Grand Tetons.

Seeing Afresh

That July we arrived in northern New Brunswick, it was cool and rainy. We had left behind daily temperatures of 100 to 105°F with no rain, so that the Umatilla River dried up except for a small trickle. In New Brunswick, a hot summer temperature would be 75°F.

I had never before seen tarpaper shacks, streets without trees, houses without flower gardens. My eyes grabbed the images, but they were difficult to understand.

The house they had promised us was not even begun. We were directed to an apartment in a row of semi-detached houses, ours being on one end. There were rudimentary furnishings to tide us over while we waited for the moving van. A couch and two easy chairs that were obviously borrowed from the hospital; office furniture; a card table and four chairs; beds for each one; a few essentials in the kitchen including four each of spoons, knives, and forks. That was it. There was a small fenced-in yard. But beyond this there was a field with wildflowers, a babbling brook, and a mountain. Imagine—wildflowers, a brook, and a mountain!

This new existence held enormous appeal for me. Why, I do not know. Perhaps it was the sparseness of it, the monastic plainness, the gritty hardness. It was the exact opposite of the life from which I had just come, and I wanted to know it, to understand it, to find home in it. I must have had an instinctive knowledge that this was reality, that I had left fantasy behind. I felt every bit as pleased with life here as I had been in my violet grove between the Silks' and Calhouns', there on the campus in Pendleton.

Daddy spoke French every day, and before summer was over we had connected with all the relatives in Lunenburg County and Cape Breton—our blood families. By November the promised little house was finished. Then winter came. Oh, how winter came! Tom and I, now aged eleven and nine, had never seen the like, and we were captivated, keen admirers of a season fresh to us. We watched the big storms with fascination, usually out in them, as school would be closed. By February the snow could be measured in yards deep, rather than feet. It was hard on top so we could walk on it, toboggan on it. As soon as we could, after supper and homework, out we'd go into the dark, black evening, lit only by stars. But such stars! Winter air, crackling with cold, provided an utterly clear sky for seeing the stars. After a few runs down the big hill behind our house, we would lie on our toboggans and see that there was no more room for any more stars in that sky—not even one more. It was that full.

It happened that during that first Maritime winter of ours, a production of Humperdinck's *Hansel and Gretel* was being mounted. Because he could act and sing and was not afraid of an audience, Tom got the part of Hansel. I was in the ballet corps, but because I watched all the rehearsals I knew the part of Gretel. And so on one of these magnificent black and starry nights, Tom and I stood on the snow-covered field, and we were Hansel and Gretel singing, "When at night I go to sleep, fourteen angels watch to keep." We stood and sang, hand in hand against the black and the unknown, and nothing has ever changed that, and those fourteen angels are still looking out for us. It was real winter, and we were Canadians. We went in for hot cocoa.

In a Field of Wildflowers

I lie in a field of wildflowers,
on the hill beside the river where
the bobolink nest and sing extravagantly.
Sweet red clover for a pillow,
a bed of purple vetch, buttercup.
Daisy, evening primrose,
with timothy to taste;
eyebright and yarrow
for social grace.
Meadow rue
for gentility,
a butterfly for honor,
a ladybug
landing on my cheek
for fun and
a July blue sky
with Monet clouds.
My day.

2 ❦ OUT OF THE BLUE
Stark Raving Clear

Ilooked out the back door, to autumn in its golden raiment, and was drawn outside. The flowers needed deadheading. I clipped dead flower heads and old seed pods into a basket. I was discouraged with the state of the blossoming of the flowers. Here it was just the middle of September, and there was precious little about for bouquets. I was growing tired of cosmos, lavatera, and calendula. I couldn't cut the purple and pink candytuft because the rockery would look sad without them. Why do the snapdragon only persist with abundant foliage when they should continue to blossom? And only one bloom at a time from the dahlia and meagre offerings from the chrysanthemum. Darn.

I would do better next year. With gardens there is always next year—a lovely thing about gardens, if one has some patience.

Something caught my eye. A peace rose. I picked it and some baby's breath and put in on the kitchen windowsill in a vase. "There. A bouquet."

The forecast came on the radio . . . warning a risk of frost.

"I think some things should be harvested," I told myself.

I got the garden cart and three baskets, filling a big one with butternut and buttercup squash, another with the remaining cucumbers and some tomatoes. My son Eric had already harvested both one basket of ripe and one of green tomatoes the previous evening. Into the third basket went the ornamental gourds. How could I have planted so many gourds? I must have had plans of decorating the whole county for Fall. I picked one small, perfect eggplant—too small, too unripe to eat, but perfect, beautiful.

I collapsed on the garden path. I was done in, legs would not move another inch. I was immobilized. Seized up. My job for the next fifteen minutes would be to lie on the grass and look at the sky, then I would have the beginning of legs again. If my life were not like this, I might not give myself up to sky-gazing. And what a sky! I don't really know what azure is, but if this is it, I can see why one might look up to see heaven. There were the most playful, soft clouds moving through this blue. These clouds were the very kind that, as a small child, I thought I could float about on, only for the want of a ladder to get up there. I would lie flat on the grass looking straight up into the sky all puffed up with clouds, and imagine what it would feel like to be up high in the clear blue. I thought clouds must be fluffy, but strong enough to hold somebody small like me. I didn't know yet the real truth, so I had the chance for lovely dreams. It did bother me, though, how I would get back down.

Suddenly a bird came into sight to break my reverie. It was far away and large. An osprey, I deduced by the wing shape and flight patterns. This fellow was just playing up there, flying close to heaven for the fun of it.

A car drove up the lane. "And me prostrate on a garden path. Oh no. Always we want to seem normal. Thank goodness, it's Elizabeth and Isabel. Friends who can understand sky-gazing."

Elizabeth Kromer is an artist. I love her work. She works with pencil crayons, which allows her to create quite unbelievable detail and extraordinary colors because she layers many colors to create the effect she wants.

Isabel is her daughter. I am learning a lot from this little girl. She has Angelman Syndrome and is physically and mentally handicapped. She was four when she started to walk. She walks unsteadily. She and I understand about balance. She doesn't speak like you or me, but she does talk with her eyes and her dear, wee face. She holds no judgment against any person, but loves without reserve. When the pediatric neurologist crassly told Elizabeth and Rob that their daughter wouldn't amount to anything, Isabel reached up and held the doctor's face in her small hands, then gave him a hug. So, I wondered—who has the handicap?

For years, Elizabeth and Rob endured doctors telling them they were in denial about Isabel's condition, because if they really understood, they would not be so cheerful. Elizabeth has always maintained it is not possible to be with Isabel and not be cheerful about her. Finally, the experts accepted the fact that these were two feisty parents who were never going to quit, that no matter the obstacle, Isabel would be given a best chance. So, against the odds and having long since passed the best-case scenario for a child with Angelman's, Isabel is going to school. I wish they could travel and share this story to give hope to other parents.

You can see why these were two people who would understand sky-gazing.

"Isabel and I have come to whisk you away! How about lunch at our house?"

"Sure!! I've been watching the sky. No legs. Come over while I get my legs back, then I'll wash up."

At Elizabeth's we surveyed her garden. Wow! Pumpkins. Huge! Elizabeth doesn't much like pumpkin. It was a mistake to plant so many. We will have to have a Jack-o'-lantern-making potluck to relieve them of this burden.

I blew bubbles for Isabel while Elizabeth heated the soup and made the coffee. A delicious lunch, then home.

After supper, Cecily and I set out to cover the best tomatoes against the frost. Near the tomatoes were some lovely borage flowers. I decided this bouquet business needed a fresh look. All I needed to do was see in a different way, and I would find a bouquet. Surely an autumn evening would be inspiration enough. Off I went.

I remembered that there were some easily accessible rowan berries on the mountain ash in the fence row heading down to the hollow. Nearby were goldenrod and Queen Anne's lace seed pods, which are lacy and creamy-colored. To this I added the borage, wild camomile, and a last few stems of veronica that had come up where I trimmed the plant in hope more would grow. I put homespun cloth on the coffee table, this unexpected beautiful bouquet, an arrangement of gourds, and the baby eggplant. I was much pleased.

Then I glanced to the piano and the drooping sunflowers in the silver pitcher. That would never do. Off again. I knew I could find a blue- and-white arrangement and made an airy bouquet of borage, white candytuft, white cosmos, baby's breath, and white potentilla.

I walked past the calendula again. In the evening light they looked more desirable. I picked the palest yellow and the brightest orange and put them in the dining room.

There! Flowers! Where I thought there were none to be had. Oh, I was pleased! Such a fine day. Such an unexpected, delightful day. I wondered who else had the job of looking at the sky.

There was no frost last night. And now today rises clear. Stark raving clear.

Out of the Blue

It was spring 1971. I had just returned from England, where I was working in London with CBC Radio, and I was bidden home for a family funeral. My brother Tom had just returned from a year's writing in the Algarve, Portugal. We engineered it so we would arrive in Toronto together, to look for housing and because I had a job at Ideas to get to. That was the first Wednesday in May. By Friday we had all but had it with the city. My colleague and friend, Jim Anderson, a senior producer of Ideas, thought it would be fun if Tom and I accompanied him, his wife Alice, and their children Gideon and Katy to Mono Mills for the weekend. Jim's parents had a farm there, which was empty in preparation for selling. So, with sleeping bags and food, we set out Friday evening.

Saturday rose full of the fresh charms of spring in the morning air and the clear, blue sky. Our friends, Robert and Janine Zend, joined us, and we got to the job at hand—turning a pasture into a landing strip for a friend of Jim's who would be arriving by plane that evening. This friend was somebody Jim had been pestering me to meet for nearly a year, but I was not enthusiastic, as Jim's description of the man seemed quite unreasonably overzealous. But for a weekend in the country, well, I couldn't see the harm.

Along the shaded edge of the woods there was still a bit of snow, which we made use of as a cooler for our lunch beer. We worked all morning filling groundhog holes and leveling the earth heaped up by the furry villains. (In Ontario there are many groundhogs.) At noon we rested by a shallow, quick-running brook, and lunched. Gideon (aged 4) and Katy (aged 2) were pretty bored, so I decided to amuse them. There was some very smooth, shiny mud along the bank of the brook, and, in spite of it being early May, the water was quite pleasant because it was shallow and ran over rocks heated by the sun. We rolled up our sleeves and pant legs and dabbled in the water, covering our exposed skin with the silky mud. We were a wonderful mess.

We got adequately cleaned off for the afternoon's activities, which meant a nap for the kids and back to the pasture-cum-landing-strip for the grown-ups, except for Zend, who managed to procure a contract watching over sleeping children, reading a book. Clever Zend. The afternoon was spent marking the field with fertilizer bags held in place by large stones, which, of course, we had to collect. Jim put a red rag on the tractor exhaust stack to act as a wind-sock, and we waited, making final improvements to any groundhog hole we thought needed it.

It had not struck me as unfortunate that I was in jeans and a white shirt for making our noontime mud packs, or that nearly waist-length fair hair cannot hide mud spatters. I thought it was a wonderful day, and how was I to know who was in the green-and-white Cessna circling about, looking over the pastoral scene, with a view to landing?

It was a picture-perfect landing. The little craft taxied up the runway toward the jolly band of onlookers, who were pleased that their work had been worthwhile. The sole occupant of the plane was the pilot. How clearly I remember. He opened the door, removing his pilot's sunglasses as he stepped out of the aircraft. He wore dark-green (pressed) pants and a light-green (pressed) shirt. That made an impression on me because we were a very motley crew by comparison. Jim introduced us to Michael Edward. Ever since that day, Tom has declared it the most perfect entrance he has ever seen!

We piled the picnic paraphernalia, tools, and ourselves into the cart that was pulled by the tractor. Katy sat on my lap. That evening there was a big bonfire, food, singing, and storytelling. Except for me. I did not tell any story, as I was struck dumb. I could not even look at this Michael man because he was so good-looking he made my eyes water.

Later, much later, when we were married, Michael said he had looked across the cart as we drove back to the house from the field and thought to himself, "I wonder if I have just met my wife."

Out of the clear blue sky . . .

Thinking About It

We were in the CBC cafeteria on Jarvis Street (Toronto) eating lunch. Zend took a piece of lined looseleaf out of his folder and made a doodle on it. There was a long black man and a round yellow woman coming down some church steps.

"It's you and Michael. You vill be marrrried!"

"For heaven's sake, Zend, this is folly—dreaming."

My friend—Robert Zend—how I loved him, and how I miss him. Zend was without a doubt the homeliest man on the face of the earth. He had wild gray hair, thinning on the top but flurried all about his face as if something terrifying had made it stand out like that. He had a very large nose, and ears that perched on the side of his head. His shoulders sloped. He was out of shape and shuffled along with the most remarkable gait. It made you wonder how he got anywhere safely. He had a thick Hungarian accent because he came to Canada as a refugee during the Revolution of 1954. He would say, "I vas a schmarrt Hungarian" (a respected, published, and well-known poet and film-maker) "and szen I became a stoopid Canadian." But not for long, Zend, not for long.

He had wonderful light-blue eyes with love in them, and a winning childlike smile, so that a few minutes after meeting him you were quite convinced he was uncommonly handsome. Before long he was a friend, colleague, uncle to me. Everybody called him "Zend," just "Zend." It suited.

I liked working with Zend because he was so full of life, a character writ large. It was like working beside a jester, a magician, a child, a poet, and a genius all in one. It drove most people crazy to work with him, but he made perfect sense to me. I liked the way he organized a series. Unique. We saw eye to eye on the logic of it, so that I was somewhat taken aback when people asked, "How can you work with him?" The two of us laughed a lot.

Funny thing, how Zend was typically very accurate about people things. He was convinced that Michael and I were the "pearrfect match." His doodle told me so. He told me to keep it "because it vas trrrue," and we went back upstairs to work. I said I would keep it, and I did. On that page of looseleaf, Zend had drawn a married couple coming down the steps of a church, music pealing, with a bit of the score in evidence, a limousine waiting, and a photographer taking pictures. The groom was tall, dark, and thin, fashioned in black marker, and the bride was a round yellow circle person. It was dated "Wednesday, October 13, 1971," and signed "Robert Zend." Michael and I were engaged on Christmas Day.

Zend's prediction bore fruit. Michael and I grew together in a bond which, on top of everything else, was a fact of our coming from homes that were committed to the same things and that had a common expression in living graciously with simplicity.

Michael's father, Graham, was the youngest son of a Scottish immigrant who left his home in Dundee and his studies at Oxford to become a farmer in Canada, where he would be allowed to marry the girl he first saw in a cherry tree on a farm in Cornwall ten years before. This would not have been permitted had he stayed in England, where such social classes did not mix. Grandfather had romantic notions about farming, which in truth was beyond him and made him bilious. Granny, on the other hand, was a superb farmer. Grandfather liked keeping beautiful gardens filled with his favorite flowers and trees. He had an extraordinary library in an otherwise typical Ontario farmhouse. When he settled into this, his own farm, his mother sent over dishes from Scotland— a place setting for sixty. Heaven knows what Great-grandmother imagined a Canadian farm was like! Nobody was ever able to explain this extraordinary set of dishes, beyond it being what is called a "banquet set" in large British homes. Everybody in the family has some of those dishes, as none ever broke.

Grandfather's biliousness disappeared when his youngest son, Graham (Michael's father), took over the little dairy farm. With his wife, Alice, they raised six children on those sixty acres. Michael is the eldest of the six. Alice was Mohawk, the great-great-granddaughter of Chief Joseph Brant. There was some concern about this mixed marriage, as it was not common in those days, but there need not have been. When Graham's family came to know Alice, they loved her without reserve. She was a concert pianist who had played at Carnegie Hall. She taught music. I came to think of her as an angel masquerading as a human being. I have known a few such women. To know them is a rare blessing.

Our common experience of living in the country, surrounded by books, music, good food, lots of visitors, and much conversation in homes grounded in faith provided the foundation, the bulwark, for a pact that went beyond any frivolous understanding of romance. We couldn't have imagined the challenges that lay ahead, but we both knew how to seize life, and this had very little to do with the conventional measure of wealth and success, a model neither of our families cared about, blessedly, for we were perched to run against the tide. It was in our nature.

It also appeared that neither Michael nor I was prepared to take marriage lightly. The statistics for marriage longevity in 1971 were not very reassuring. And so, I sat at the table in my Toronto room on Roxborough Street making a sober, thoughtful list, while unbeknownst to me Michael sat at his desk in Brantford making another sober, thoughtful list. The lists were titled "What I want from life." We wrote the same list.

Our life together has been, is being, the first best adventure. The lists were true. How glad I am that I eventually had the nerve to look at him.

After we were married in New Brunswick, Michael's parents threw a big party for us at the Holiday Inn in Brantford, for the Ontario friends and relatives. The Zends, of course, came. Father had decided we should have some fun and that square dancing would fit the bill, and a "Caller" was duly added to the party roster. It was perfect, as everybody joined in with enthusiasm. Zend and Janine were in a "square" with Michael and me, which also included my brother Tom and his first wife, Cathy, and Michael's sister Allyson and her husband Walt. I thought we would hurt ourselves laughing as Zend made his way through the do-si-do, allemande left, bow to your partner, and such.

"But vy do youu call it sqvvvuare dancing vhen everrieboody iss going around in cyircles?" asked a very entertained Zend.

He loved it, and of course he loved it that he amused us. When we visited Zend and Janine with children in tow, they adored him. They wanted to be related to him. "Mom, is Zend our uncle?" What child would not want such an uncle? I told them we were related in the heart.

Meadow Ice

I fell in meadow and forgot.
I fell in the snow and remembered.
I cannot move.

      Does mercy melt icicles to
      make way for violets?

If I roll over in the meadow
there are primrose, daisy, cornflower.
If I roll over in the snow there are
a thousand-thousand diamonds.

3 🦎 PEARSIE

It was a tumble-down, one-hundred-and-fifty-year-old house looking to the Pinette River on a hundred acres of rural calm. It suited us. The house was showing its years, but it was solid Maritime Vernacular, and when you have no money you can't be picky. There were pretty pictures from every window—meadow, forest, river, orchard. It seemed a good place for having a family. So we said yes, took it, and named it Pearsie Farm after the original family farm in Scotland and its offshoot homestead in Ontario. The landscape changes with the seasons so that there is always a new visual treat surrounding us.

The summer before we settled in here, we had traveled to the Maritimes to attend a wedding and have a holiday. The holiday included a brief stop on Prince Edward Island to see friends and because I wanted Michael to see my Island. Well, he fell in love with it instantly because it "felt like home." That's what he said. And he was a farm boy who wanted a farm. Our first little home was the hired man's house on Long Lane Farm just outside Brantford. While living there, we traveled the back roads of Brant County, but the possibility of owning land there was out of the question for us. A million dollars would buy us a few acres. We were penniless. But we were not stupid, and we could see that the dream of recreating the Ontario Pearsie where Michael grew up, with a Pearsie II, was feasible on the Island.

We decided that whoever got a job here first would take it. That would have to be me, since Michael was teaching in Brantford and committed till the end of the school year. The hard part was that my new job began in February, which meant a long winter and spring separated by half a very large country. I stayed with a dear, beloved friend in Charlottetown, Sherry Finley, so at least I wasn't alone all that time. Sherry became an integral part of our family and a "Nammy" to our children.

Two days after I got to the Island, I started looking for a place to rent in the country, thinking that would give us lots of time to look around and eventually find a place to buy. There wasn't anything in the country to rent, but the real estate agent thought I should look at a farm that was for sale in Belfast. For some reason I agreed to go have a look.

We trudged across a snow-covered field to get to the house. The lane was impassable. But I liked this farm. Old. Classic Maritime. I had no idea the property had remnant Acadian forest and that it was exceptional. I had no idea there were trout in the river, but I liked the river, too. It was frozen over and looked like a good place to skate. And the house . . . it had the strong lines of a traditional Island farmhouse, with such possibilities, but such a mess! Forgetting we were planning to have a family, I did not bother to look into the school situation. I wasn't there in my mind just yet. I had no idea there was an excellent elementary/junior high four miles down the road—a school which, just as Michael was available, needed someone who could teach the unusual combination of music and physical education. There was a library to build up, and teams to coach and choirs to direct. Music festivals, track meets, concerts, science fairs, drama festivals. While vice-principal, he taught junior-high English, science, and math. When he became principal, he saw it as an honor, for he considered his staff "the dream team of teachers." There is a vast lawn around the school for playing, and woods at the back for making discoveries. If you look out the expansive windows of Belfast School, on a clear day you will see across the Northumberland Strait to Nova Scotia, all the way to the hills of Cape Breton. On hot days in June, teachers can take the children to the beach.

I called Michael, described the farm to him, and proposed it might be prudent to make an offer. The price was irresistible. There were no others even like it. There was talk of land prices rising soon. For such a price we could have purchased a postage-stamp-sized lot in Brantford with nothing on it, I said. I remember what I said because it was an understatement: "The house needs a little spit and polish, but it has possibilities and the property is lovely with fields and river and woods!" He agreed. It was decided. My plan was worth a try. One problem remained—the penniless part.

I marched into the real estate office, just as if I knew what I was doing, and made an offer to rent for six months, with first option to buy at the end of the six months and all the rent money going to the down payment. This would mean Michael could see the place when he came to visit during March break, we could experience the land in summer, and we'd have six months to gather together a down payment and wouldn't be out anything. They accepted the offer. The property had been on the market for the better part of a year. It was the mess of the house that worked to our advantage. Other people had been interested, but couldn't get past the dogged work it would need. But this is PEI, and word does travel, and so a couple who had been interested in the farm galvanized when they heard there was another interested party. These people walked into the real estate office with cold, hard cash just ten minutes after I left. The real estate agent said, "We have just accepted an offer." God bless that man!

For the farm, I banked everything I made beyond the rent and what I insisted Sherry take for board. It was hard to get her to take anything. Michael, too, was vigorously saving. All my spare time was spent at the farm making it decent for my dear husband, who was to come in March when we would celebrate our first anniversary. My friend Kent Stetson, with whom I worked at OFY (Opportunities for Youth, a Secretary of State employment program), and who was a close college buddy, helped a lot. It was he who helped me shovel six inches of petrified doggie doo-doo from the basement floor. It was a dirt floor, being that the house was an antique and set upon a stone foundation. Squatters, who inhabited the house for some months, had allowed dogs to use it as a giant litter-box. I looked at that job, then went up to Cooper's Store and bought a pair of overalls. (Twenty-six years later, those overalls still existed in a somewhat battered form and, seen to be a desirable fashion piece, were then adopted by a teenage nephew. Eventually, I got a new pair of overalls at Cooper's.)

By the time Michael arrived, the house looked presentable. He liked it, and he loved the land. He didn't think I was completely mad. It was a gorgeous March break, and we looked forward to seeing the farm in summer.

I flew to Ontario in May so we could pack up the little house that had been our first home. We rented a moving van and off we went—Jim (the very Jim who introduced us), Michael, me, and Nancy, our cat, who was sedated. The evening we drove off the ferry and onto the Island it was stunningly beautiful. May was showing off. In a golden evening light, the Island was completely serene and calm in its gentle pastoral freshness. There was a sense that the place was loved and cared for.

Since March, I had painted and papered and polished and scrubbed, so that the house was gradually undergoing a transformation. With our possessions unpacked, it was pretty cozy by the time Michael and Jim had to leave at the end of the long weekend. I can only imagine what a painful moment it was for Michael to return to Ontario with the empty truck, while his wife and new home waited behind for a further reunion at the end of the school year. After he left, I continued my quest to make our home inviting. I credited Beethoven for getting me through the long hours I worked alone on the house, as I'd turn up one of the symphonies rather loudly and forge ahead. I needed music that was tough, determined, and single-minded. When I finished a project and stopped to admire my handiwork, I'd restore my serenity with Mozart.

On Canada Day, my love returned. I had picked wild strawberries for a special treat. I wanted to have flowers planted around the house to greet him. We had forgotten to take our garden tools out of the garage when we packed up in May, so I had used kitchen implements, a large carving knife and big serving spoon, to make flowerbeds right around the house. It was quite a chore! It looked so much more welcoming to have some flowers to greet him, because the rest of the yard was pretty bare, except for trees.

By the time our six months were up, we were in love with the place. We had time to discover many of its delights, though more were yet to come with autumn and winter. At that time, country property was considered a particular sort of risk, and so required a down payment equal to one-third of the cost of the property. We had been saving every penny since March. We cashed out Michael's retirement because he was leaving the Ontario system, and we sold my dear car, my sun-yellow Volkswagen Beetle, little Beatrice. I always regretted that, but we wouldn't have netted much from the sale of the other car—a very ordinary Vega—and, besides, the hatchback allowed us to use the car as a truck. Lord knows we had lots of truckin' to do! Whenever I see a yellow Beetle, I remember that mine helped buy this homestead, and I am not so regretful after all.

That was my one and only foray into the world of real estate, but it was the one that counted.

We worked very hard that summer and every summer, fall, winter, and spring since. This place is evidence of a lot of work, and how satisfying and educational it has been. Imagine all that we have learned—about work that required new skills, and about ourselves. It turned out even better than the dream we had when we sat over tea in the little house at Long Lane Farm, imagining we would have our own farm one day.

We love it here. We have invested our sweat and our dreams in the place. It is ours. Pearsie is the spirit of place for us, and as we all grow and change it remains the constant physical reality for us. And here is where we've had our family. Father, mother, children. It started out with Michael and me and then babies into children into young adults and now back to Michael and me, as the children are grown and heading off on their own, sometimes home and sometimes away. But we're still here, Michael and I. We know there will be babies and children again, another generation, joy yet to arrive! Flowers on the dining room table, after-supper walks down the back lane, to the Cove and through the woods. How we've loved those walks. Always different, always new, always the same.

If this place is a blessing, it is because something happens here. It is not simply a piece of real estate that draws anyone close. True, the landscape is winning, but it is the nature of our commitment to one another as a family, here in our home, that offers something tangible to share, to learn, to grow. Michael and I cleave to each other. "Cleave": I love that word, so full of so many layers of holding.

It seems a small thing, this homely life, but maybe it isn't. Pearsie became the ark for our adventure. Nobody ever said charting the course would mean calm seas all the way. In fact, I think we hit a rogue wave! Tom told me about rogue waves. His schooner, *Avenger*, hit a trio of them sailing in the North Atlantic from Newfoundland to Nova Scotia. There was wind, and sun, too, when forty-foot waves rose suddenly, out of nowhere, tossing the boat 180° upside-down, into the sea. By some miracle, they survived. They sailed home. Sometimes, I feel we hit our own version of a rogue wave. One of us has MS. Sometimes I am turned upside-down. Both of us share the course. Grab the tiller, Michael, I'm wobbly and the wind is strong.

He does. With a firm grip and face to the spray and my hand in his, we continue on. He never once has shown disappointment in me. I know he worries about me and becomes over-protective when I am unwell. I am sure it is confusing to stand by and watch. Still, he never lets me stop dreaming, never lets me think that there is no way to re-think an old dream. Together, we learned about mourning something important that has gone. Neither of us was sure how to go about it, but we'd have to try, so we could move forward. I cried my tears, then faced the unknown. Then we turned strong to meet the day. The sun kept rising. There was no other choice.

We are up for sunrise, so early. Is it this fresh glimpse of heaven that enthrals me? Or his brown eyes that gift me with strength for a new day?

On our wedding day Tom sang me a gift written and composed for his little sister. It began like this:

> *So you found someone to share your life*
> *One to make you laugh and cry,*
> *the way we used to do.*
> *And I can see he's equal to the task*
> *for all the things inside of him*
> *are written over you.*
> *And your love song will be beautiful,*
> *your love song will be true,*
> *your love song will be everything,*
> *for your love song is you.*

Once it has been sung, a song is forever.

The Eyes

A lways it takes place when I am working in the kitchen. He approaches from behind and places his hands firmly on my shoulders and jiggles me. Whatever I am doing, I can't do, because I shake with this imposed tremor. I may get lifted straight up in the air like a mannequin being moved or carried in his arms around and around. There isn't a lot I can do because he is six-foot-two, and I am five-foot-five. He has the advantage. Then I am returned to solid ground and given a hug, and with a satisfied grin he announces, "There. Mom is cured. Don't you feel better? See—no more Parkinson's." (Parkinson's would be shakier than my MS.) "See how much better you feel. Couldn't even peel a carrot before, and now see how steady you are. You got the cure! Parkinson's all gone. Good little Mom."

By the time the cure is effected I am laughing because it is funny, and the accompanying banter gets me, in spite of myself. Moments of silliness to forget the seriousness. Eric and Cecily say, "Mom, don't let him do that to you!"

"Gethin, leave Mom alone! You'll hurt her!"

"No, I won't hurt her. I am giving her the cure. I'm making her better. See how glad she is. She's got to have the cure. You have to know how the cure works."

"Mom, make him stop!"

Working in the kitchen is a definite sign one is on the mend, back in the thick of things. This was the exacerbation that was the beginning of everybody's understanding of how MS can present itself in grim reality. I understood the importance of Gethin's cure. Everybody thought it was disrespectful, except Gethin and me, and eventually I convinced him to revamp the cure so it would not worry his siblings. I've never asked him to stop altogether because, just now, I need it. If you looked into his eyes you would know why.

Having MS is hard. Know that. Hard for me, and for my husband, and my children. I cannot dwell in the regions of everyone's pain for very long because it hurts like an explosion in my heart. A mother is the one who begins as everything to a child. In the beginning there is no sense of personhood apart from mother. Baby and mother are one. Gradually, baby comes to know self and moves apart. What an amazing thing, watching a little one grow into a particular, marvellous, interesting person.

And always this extraordinary bond because I carried them and bore them and nurtured them at my breast, and my arms were their womb with a view. If they hurt, I hurt twice—once for them and once for me. Mothers know most everything (a child's "everything"), and when you need something you only need to ask Mother. Where safety dwells.

How must it feel to a child when Mother becomes ill with an illness that will not go away, one that is unpredictable and scary? I have MS, and I wonder how it feels to my children, how it really feels. It doesn't matter how old they are, how grown-up or how immature. Something has changed, and I cannot fool myself that it hasn't. I shall never again know a carefree moment. When I cannot be relied upon to do and do again, they must rely upon themselves and do for me, too. What I once did, I cannot, not always. Sometimes yes, sometimes no. Not dependably. What I can do today, will I be able to do tomorrow, or will there come some new tyranny to my body? Where is the safety now? In whose arms? How will they look upon my many, peculiar symptoms? Is my illness an impediment to their need to find their own space or to be just kids, sometimes big and sometimes small, sometimes old and sometimes young? Is this a burden too great? Who am I to my children now? Safety or fear? Or is this our greatest chance to grow? Is this new cement in the bond? An unexpected dimension of love? Mine and theirs.

I have tried to see it through each of their eyes. Gethin comes home from college, and I am unwell and grow worse and worse till a full-blown exacerbation has me in its grips. My first really big show. He is not sad or downhearted. If he is afraid he doesn't show it. He has enormous faith and an unshakable knowledge that there is nothing to fear. His approach is to see that I laugh, to show me I must never forget to laugh, that there is something amusing most days, and a smile beats a frown every time. Mirth. And so the cure. An affectionate, zany way of telling me over and over again that I am his own Mom, "the best Mom I ever had."

"Gethin, I'm the only Mom you've ever had."

"Doesn't matter. You're still the best Mom I ever had," no matter what. While he swings me around the kitchen, everybody else might think it is disrespectful, but he knows and I know it is a mask for both our pain, a way of saying he understands. I've looked in his eyes after I get the cure and it is not disrespect, but rather, "I'm with you, Mom," and "little Mom" is not a put-down but a declaration that he will watch out for me and protect me.

It is my dance. My heart dance. My love dance. My first-son dance. There is a peaceful comfort in him I treasure. He has the most extraordinarily beautiful eyes.

My Girl

I love having a daughter. The female view is different from the male view; of course, that is the point. It is a blessing having another female in the house. A daughter knows girl things from the start, and there is no telling any but a girl how it works, this female perspective and talent. Cecily grew up in a world of boys. It was the luck of the draw—brothers, cousins, neighbors—all boys. Hers—the feisty, hearty, give-it-all-you've-got-I-can-do-anything nature—fit in well with this boy world. When necessary, she escaped them to her girl things. "I need a break from those guys!" So when her mother was incapacitated, well, was it any wonder that, like a mother, she answered with her heart?

One summer I was held captive in my Treehouse. This Treehouse is not in a tree. It is in a house, our house, our bedroom. In this space, there is lots of light and wind and green, with windows on three sides. Fragrance of lilac, fresh-cut hay, or new-mown grass drifts in the windows. Bird song wakes us and peepers sing in the evening. Crickets and cicadas make their exhilarating, sometimes annoying, summer refrain. I think it is a room with the imagination of a treehouse, particularly when one can go no further in the world. When an exacerbation hit me like a thunderclap, I retreated to regard life from this place. Having one's world shrink so dramatically, and so fast, would feel very confining if the reason for the shrinkage did not cause one to appreciate the change in the size of one's world. Suddenly, a small world felt exactly right. It is generally good to be in the size of world one can manage. I expected to resent this modified prospect of opportunity, but it was a relief, a safe place to be. It was exactly what I could negotiate. It felt safe. There wasn't any other place I dared to be, and, waiting there, I could go anywhere in my imagination. I went many places that summer, by myself. One day, I'd get out. I knew that. I hoped it would not take too long.

That summer, watching life from my Treehouse, I watched, too, my fifteen-year-old daughter take on the role of Chatelaine of Pearsie. There were meals cooked—delicious—day after day. She tended the house, laundry, garden, and looked after our summer company. My Sess. (She was named after her Great-grandmother Sess, so that "Cecily" becomes "Sess." She is well-named, for her foremother, too, had a strong, big spirit.) There was an awesome summer camp (what else could you call it?) being run for her little cousins. Croquet, frisbee elimination, rowing, walks to the woods, trips to the beach, running games, board games, laughing and singing and carrying on. It gave Aunt Erica and Uncle Vic a rest. And she organized her work team . . . I could hear her brothers being given their marching orders as the work was divvied up. Somebody had to make these things happen. It is what a mother does, but hers was in bed. I was so very proud of her, and touched that she would take all this on.

On the outside she was all business and action. I might see from the window her entourage (all in life jackets, Cecily carrying the oars, heading down to the river), or partake of meals delivered to me on a tidy tray, but I was not told about the inside. On the inside there was a different story. Not a word said to me, ever, about those things she carried around, the concern, the worry. Nobody expressly gave her the load she picked up, but had she not bent to carry it, I expect she knew it would not get done. A woman knows how to make the daily business of life happen. And she was just a girl—an incredibly capable, kind girl. I wondered if she knew it was a gift? I think not yet. I missed her that summer, because I knew about the inside. She was too busy being Martha to have much Mary time, and I doubt she felt very Mary-ish for me.

Where was her mother? Her real other mother?

I had no legs. My eyes were too blurry to read, speech was difficult, and so was swallowing, and the journey of fork from plate to mouth was a long and treacherous one. I was forced to live inside. Inside my head. Inside my heart. Inside my Treehouse. I learned how much harder it is to receive than to give. I wanted to cry out that it was not any easier for me to do nothing while she did all, than it was for her to do all. My thanks could never say exactly what I felt. I didn't know if she understood that. What I was feeling on the inside was likely pretty close to what she was feeling on the inside, but in reverse. I still had a lot more to learn. And how would I ever be able to make this up to my daughter? I was still her real mother. Eventually I'd understand how. Would she?

Some years have passed and a photo taken that summer of Cecily with her cousin Victor in her arms rides on our fridge door. How he has grown since that other summer. Sess said, when she first saw the picture there, "I love that picture—it tells exactly how I feel about Vic, how much I love him." She bonded with him the summer of her awesome camp. She might not realize it, but that is what happened. When you give in love, there is a reward. I love that picture, too. It is how I feel about her.

We are incredibly close, my daughter and I. We can curl up in bed most any day and talk for hours. We share life unabashedly, delight in each other's company, share each other's sadness and triumph, miss each other when apart. I know now it was not a case of my making it up to her because, in the end, we made it up to each other. Gift given, gift received. Love given, love received. All is forgiven.

While I was in the Treehouse they told me she kept flowers on the dining room table, just like usual. And always dessert and tea. Everyone loves to be around her. She sparkles. The sparkle is what finds its way from her heart to her eyes.

Cheeks

The door would fling open, and a small, irresistibly cute boy (large brown eyes, curly dark hair, perpetually pink cheeks, chubby knees) would stand there and loudly proclaim, "Mom! Mom!" (twice in case he couldn't see me), "I love you!" That was the message. It was delivered, so the door would slam, and out he'd go. This happened regularly throughout the day when they were outdoors playing. Such a message! Some things never change. "Mom! I love you!" is how Eric has approached life with me, and he has not changed his story. He loves to be outdoors. He has never lost those pink cheeks. I am not surprised he turned out to be the one with a gardener's heart.

It was winter, frozen and February. Eric and I were sitting by the warmth of the living room stove. He was finishing high school, and his siblings were away at college, so it was just the three of us that year.

"Let's plan the garden. I have some ideas," he offered. We often talked gardening. He disappeared, returning with an armload of gardening books. He gets very technical. He worked summers at a tree nursery. Comfortable with plants, he took a bold, unafraid approach. "I think we need to move things around—perennials, shrubs—and make order in the herb garden. Raised beds would be good. Things are out of control. We're losing visual impact because plants don't show properly." (It's his artist's eye. He paints, too.) "I'll help. We'll work together. Let's do it, Mom. It would be fun." I must have been looking doubtful. "Work with me on this, Mom. Don't worry, I'll be your legs. With things tidied up, it will be easier for you to manage." He was leafing through the books. "Look at these grasses. Great for variety of texture in foliage. I wish I had buckets of money. Wouldn't it be great to be able to buy whatever we wanted? We should start the things we want from seed. You can use my window." (A big south-facing window.) "Is Dad going to do something to the irises this year?" The irises are his Dad's particular pleasure, some brought from his grandfather's garden. "Let's make a list. Where are the gardening catalogues?"

It's a nice way to spend February evenings.

The ground thawed, warmed, and dried till it was arable and ready for us. Eric put on my canvas gardening hat (my best hat), gathered our equipment from the barn, and we set to in the weedy herb garden. A Ho-Mi for Eric, a Ho-Mi for me. (We can't imagine how we did such work before these wonderful hoes arrived on the scene. A simple, perfect tool for the job.) And there was a lot of weeding to do, too. He stuck with it, after school and on weekends, till it was finished. I worked during the days as much as hands and legs allowed. Then we stood back and admired our work. With the satisfied look of a steward who loves the land, Eric said, "Isn't that so good, Mom?"

I was looking at him, and it was just what I was thinking.

Now he is away at college, thriving. I got an e-mail from a dear friend who happens to be a professor at King's University. It was a very short e-mail, but it said everything. It read: "I saw Eric on Friday. He radiates Happiness."

It was Eric who said, "Mom, I can't wait to read what you are writing!" Soft, brown eyes with rosy cheeks that melted into his heart. Eric-love. And when he helps me, always a smile.

Hanging Lavender

Time to harvest my belle lavender,
the fragrance of Provence,
I travel in an armload of perfume.

It hangs to dry from a pine beam,
to make sweet lavender pomanders,
full of summer thoughts, tender mornings:
bare feet and coffee on the porch,
hummingbird on delphinium.

On the serious side of the season,
change is my luminous portion,
where summer gives to autumn,
wind circles into winter:
coffee served in a slower dawn,
warmth from the fire in the stove.

Lavender lingers in the linen chest,
and I wonder if the hummingbird
is safe in South America.

4 ❧ MAGNIFICENT SPLENDOR

Walking in the woods in my new suit of MS, I was given an insight into the fabric of this garment of mine. My MS suit's lining is not of that familiar carefree sort we like. It is rough, makes each day different to me, unfamiliar, alien. In this way, my suit effects a distinguished air, for it sets each day apart from the ordinary.

This day, it was necessary to go to the woods, a good place for thinking. When I am in the woods, my thoughts drift all around.

Wherever you look in the forest, something has happened or is happening. Fox droppings reveal white fur in the mix, the fur of a snowshoe hare in wintertime. The spring forest floor is covered in wild lily of the valley with its sweet, light fragrance, very different from the much admired fragrance of classic lily of the valley, but every bit as exciting to encounter. Both these flowers are white. Through the trees, a blue sky with clouds floating in it. There are a lot of white things to see in the green, green shade.

This day, the white-throated sparrow sang, so I sat to listen to its splendid song. And I thought about white. Clouds. Snow. Moon. Moby Dick. Eyeballs. Easter lilies. Seashells. White clarity in a sparrow's song and, sometimes, if one is lucky, in a choir's song. Imagine something that cannot be seen, only heard, yet described precisely, as color. Only white could be the color to describe pure sound. I see there is much more in everything than it first seems. Like in Narnia, the inside is bigger than the outside. I realized: there was something more inside my MS, and one day I'd figure it out.

Realizing I had uncovered a significant fact in an examination-for-discovery of my MS, I felt that multiple sclerosis was a terrible name for a disease. It is accurate, true, but dreadfully pedantic. As the official name for my disease, I was stuck with it, but for my own imaginative intentions, there had to be something better.

Multiple sclerosis. It is like this: imagine nerve fibres as a bundle of insulated electric wires though which an impulse must pass, in order for instructions to be delivered to the body. Should the insulation wear out, electricity will have a devil of a time getting to the place it wants to go, and the job will not get done, without a drain on the power grid, if ever. That's exactly how it is with MS. Bundles of nerve fibres are insulated with myelin. For some peculiar reason, the body attacks itself, and holes are created in this myelin sheath, preventing messages from traveling from the brain to their destination. Legs, arms, hands, eyes cannot work, balance is off, sensations are confused, not to mention the exhaustion of trying to send information though a bad wire, so the body is overwhelmingly fatigued. Sometimes these holes repair. Sometimes they do not, and so, scars are formed. These are called sclerosis, and because nobody ever gets just one, the condition is called multiple sclerosis, many scars. How is that for a moniker?

I hated it from the outset. Because I had a feeling that I was going to know something beyond many scars, I wished my disease had a better name. Suspecting that eventually some truth would be revealed to me (in the living of it), that this MS affair was not going to be a waste of my time, I needed something that offered promise, even if that promise turned out to be an obstinate one.

I am almost certain it couldn't mean anything to anyone but me, but I much prefer having the Magnificent Splendor rather than Multiple Sclerosis. Here, optimism, adaptability, humor, and beauty are vastly more tangible. Also, it doesn't sound nearly so dismal. Imagine if I could say, if I were brave enough, "I have the Magnificent Splendor!" Wouldn't people be amazed! I think it would have a rather different result than saying, "I have Multiple Sclerosis," which causes people to wince.

If I had a dog, I'd call it Mya-Lyn. Mylee for short. It would be a big dog and would fetch things for me.

The Wasp Nest

Some wasps made a beautiful nest on the wild rose bush near the croquet pitch. I watched it all summer, and there was nobody home so it must have been last year's effort. It is a perfect wasp nest, in foggy gray and wisps of silvery white with a weed growing right through it. The grasshoppers have amused themselves sunning on top of it. There is definitely nobody home. It is a perfect *objet d'art*. And I want it to keep.

Nobody wanted to help me rescue the wasp nest for art's sake, since they all thought there must be somebody home. Well, I'd get it myself.

I did. It was a bit of a ticklish task since the rose bush is so thorny, and my legs are shaky and my hands unpredictable. Ah! but I got it. I put it in the big crockery jug where it looked just fine with rose hips on the branches. Later, for Christmas, I added Canadian holly, which annoyed everyone, except me, since it kept dropping its berries. In the spring I threw out the holly and put in pussy willows. Come summer I wondered if it might be a good idea to set my prize on the porch, for interest's sake, but the thought crossed my mind that lazy wasps might take up residence in this ready-made home.

A wasp nest is a perfectly wonderful creation. Layers and layers of fragile paper-thin comb form a house of immense practicality, yet profound delicacy. Tenacity put it together. I have been attempting to understand why this house of gray holds my attention so. Just look at it! I think I feel a kinship of purpose with this nest, for I, too, have created a nest. It is what mothers do. Nobody else can replace my effort, my joy, my position in our nest. It is perfectly our nest. A home of immense practicality, yet profound delicacy. Like the wasp nest there are layers of foggy grayness—the relentless, repeated acts of taking care and making order. The things that must be done, always the same and always forgotten the moment they are accomplished, boring if I don't remember this is love at work. These are the wisps of silvery white, the light that points to somewhere else and is never forgotten. Love given. Love received. The celebration. The sparkle. Arrows toward heaven. I revel in this job. I am irreplaceable. There have been other jobs, of necessity, where one is important, so they say. In all those I have been replaced. Now, by necessity, I am here in the nest I love. Nothing—not time, nor illness, nor age can prevent the silvery wisps from growing wider and brighter because we have built this nest in love. I don't care what the world thinks.

Immense practicality, yet profound delicacy. This is my best effort.

Two Novembers

I like November. I like it for its honesty, its stark, unadorned honesty. It has nothing to hide. It has given everything. Creation empties itself for us. November never disappoints. April and May are in peril of greatly disappointing us because our need is great, and sometimes April and May cannot meet our need. November is gray, windy, and chilly. You can depend upon that. It stands as a brave, lonely, unadorned sentinel between the riotous color of autumn and the cozy comforts of winter.

Here I am in the hospital. It is November 1996. My bed is beside a window. Outside it is, of course, gray, windy, and chilly. It rains lightly. I am in the only bed there was available in the hospital, in a ward with three other women. I am in the bed nearest the bathroom. I noticed that right away and was glad because I can only walk short distances. I have trouble getting my slippers on, so I will go there in my sock feet if the floor is not too slippery. It is something to think about. The bed is high. Awkward. Across from me is an elderly woman with a heart condition. She is delightfully Irish and sparkly. Beside her is another elderly woman, also with a heart condition, but deaf. She can't hear me from way over there. She has a sweet, knowing smile. Beside me is a young woman with a stomach condition that befuddles everyone. She has lost 60 pounds in several months. They had better figure out what her trouble is soon. There is not much left of her.

I arrived at the ward with Elizabeth driving the wheelchair at top speed. Elizabeth said she couldn't imagine what possessed her to think there was any rush to get me from Admissions to the Floor. I think it was the message I had received earlier, "If you can get here by noon we will have a bed for you." And so there we were—me in a wheelchair, one with no footrest, trying to keep my feet up as Elizabeth pushed at an enthusiastic pace. (She later had dreams about wheeling me at breath-taking speeds through the hospital.) It was amusing. I am grateful she was able to bring me into town on short notice. I couldn't have pulled Michael out of school to rush me to the hospital to claim this one elusive bed.

I hadn't planned to be in the hospital. Till now, I've only been in the hospital to have babies, which was good. However, during the second week in November I felt a marked increase in a fundamental "unwellness" that was exhibiting itself as a growing, gnawing fatigue, a stiffness of sorts in the trunk, a heavy right leg, a tight band—beginning as a belt at the waist. During the autumn I had the unmistakable feeling that "something was in the wings," rather like the sensation of walking by a gaggle of ten-year-old boys equipped with a pile of snowballs. One knows one is going to get it. The question is when.

By mid-November the exploding dart-gun headaches established themselves in a pattern of one explosion approximately every two minutes. This was tolerable, as in the past I had experienced more intense manifestations of the darts, and at two-second intervals. Next the tight band extended to include my entire torso and increased significantly in intensity. My right leg turned into hemlock, my old companion, tree leg. The cardboard feeling on the soles of both feet intensified, and there was numbness to mid-calf. My hands also became more numb than usual, which, of course, had a noticeable effect on fine motor control.

Shortly after this I scrawled in my notebook that I was numb from collarbone to toes, including my arms. In previous sessions, I had been numb only from midriff down. The headache was unrelenting. Two extra-strength Tylenol provided two hours' relief, yet I had no desire to move to anything stronger, as codeine causes that dreaded constipation, which (while I could tolerate the headaches) I considered the greater of the discomforts. As the entry point of the dart was at a 45° angle above and behind my ear, my inner ear began to feel a peculiar pain, and this in both ears, though more intensely in the left ear. My skull, at the entry points, was tender to the touch.

I was incredulous, dismayed, and insulted by these events. "I can't be immobilized now. Christmas is coming. There are things to do!" Although I suppose I should better describe the feeling as pride (oh, fool!), the notion that nobody in the family could be a Christmas magician as good as I.

I called Dr. Barbara Flanagan. We agreed on a course of Solu-Medrol. I had a belief, unfounded on anything but vanity, that I would be up and about, if only for a course of steroids. I calculated the risks and side effects. Based on the success of some past experiences with Solu-Medrol and conveniently forgetting the failures, and losing patience with my rapidly increasing discomfort, I decided to go ahead and get the treatment. Were Christmas not so close I might have waited it out. With Michael teaching and me unable to drive, it would be impossible for me to get to the hospital for the daily intravenous treatments. Dr. Flanagan moved quickly, and, thus, I was admitted to the Queen Elizabeth Hospital in Charlottetown at noon. All I could think of was being a drain on the medical system.

I was numb from the chin down. So what could I do? Dealing with small things like buttons or earrings was impossible, as was fastening a bra at the back, and brushing my teeth with the aim of getting less toothpaste on my forehead than on my teeth. Holding cutlery so that the food did not spill before I got it to my mouth was a trial. I could walk short distances. I could not write. My speech was fine. That pleased me. It is so humiliating to be unable to speak clearly. Also my eyes were good so I could read, though it was hard to hold a book and page-turning was tricky. I had brought several with me. *Ship of Fools* by Katherine Anne Porter, *All Hallows' Eve* by Charles Williams, and an anthology of poetry. I was not sure what made good hospital reading. It came down to which book was easiest to grasp.

The hospital was full. Hot. Dry. Whoever thought of the brilliant idea of sealing the windows? I wondered how patients survive any time at all in such uncommonly hard beds. I had a fitful sleep. I thought a shower would refresh me. The shower room was just across the hall and, in there, a special chair, a sort of wheelchair, to sit in while showering. Surely that would be relaxing. I decided to give it a try. But my hands didn't work. The soap was slippery, and it slithered out of my hand straight away. I could do this, I could. As I reached down for the soap, I fell out of the chair. There I sat, with the chair on my head, the soap ever-elusive. It was nothing but a greasy circus. I gathered together every ounce of decorum I could and did the whoopsie shuffle back to my room. (Do the "whoopsie shuffle" as follows: drag feet in a shuffle, shuffle; say

"Whoops. Sorry," as you bump something or someone . . .) What a treacherous thing a shower can be.

It was so busy in the hospital that I felt great empathy for the nurses who bustle endlessly. Still, so cheerful and willing. But always, there were serendipitous blessings to be found. My roommates were very dear. We shared some good talks, hearty laughs, and sympathetic support for one another. I canceled my request for a private room. I enjoyed my roommates in spite of the fact they all snored. So I worked hard to fall asleep. Hospital noises seemed louder after visiting hours were over and it was time for bed. The pillow was hot. There was a plastic case under the pillow slip. I hated that. Instead of counting sheep, I entertained myself with a rerun in my head. It was that other November when I began this strange journey . . .

On a typical cold, gray 1990 November afternoon I rushed out of my office in Dalton Hall to run across the University of Prince Edward Island campus to fetch material from the library. I nearly left without my coat, but, remembering the weather, grabbed it as I left my office. When I hit the cold air I was stunned by the feeling that one entire side of my body was burning hot. It was as though a plumbline had been dropped from the center of my forehead marking the precise center of my body. My left side felt on fire as it hit the cold air, as though it was not air at all, but hot oil. As soon as I entered the library the hotness faded somewhat, only to reappear when I went back outside to return to my office.

By the time I got home from work that evening, my legs were extremely sensitive to touch. Direct contact with anything was very painful, so I went to bed with pantyhose on as a barrier between me and the rest of the tactile world. Dr. Flanagan said to wait forty-eight hours to see if shingles developed. They did not. The left half of my torso was now numb.

I missed one day of work, which was a day for the hot to simmer down. After a couple of weeks, as the numbness persisted while the heat was fading, I had a neurological examination. The doctor, who was not a neurologist (because PEI did not have one), felt "it could be MS, though it might be a neurological virus due to stress." He told me that, since there was neither a cure nor a treatment for MS, I should not overly concern myself. I should track my symptoms for a year-and-a-half or two years, and then there would be a clinical indication of MS.

Of course, I was convinced it was the stress-related virus. When I left this doctor's office I proceeded to Dr. Cottreau's to have a lump on my breast examined. Of the two examinable sets of symptoms, this worried me more. Dr. Cottreau happily assured my I had fibroid cyst disease that was of no concern and that would disappear, later, in menopause. Great. I had a condition for which the cure is menopause. But blessedly no cancer in a cancer-prone family. This was a relief. He was, though, very concerned about the numbness, "much more concerned about the numbness." These were words I would remember again and again, because he is a doctor for whom I have great respect, and he had "that look" on his face . . . the one that doctors get, that tells a lot.

During Christmas holidays I had my first experience with dart-gun headaches. The dart struck at two-second intervals behind my right ear. Over several weeks these utterly unusual, indescribable, and very painful sensations made their way in a path down and around my neck and finally "out" my chin and were gone. Accompanying the headaches came a numbness on the right side of my face and shoulder, as well as my right hand and, eventually, my entire arm. I remember lying on the couch reading some of the new Christmas books, thinking how curious a thing this was. By February it was impossible to write. I typed everything, even phone messages at the office. I couldn't ski because my legs were weak when in the cold, and there was a fierce pain down my shin when I was on my skis. By March the symptoms began to fade, and by April it was nothing more than a strange memory. I was completely well. Not only that, but Michael discovered the serviceman missed a hole in the firebox when he cleaned the furnace in the late fall. After a call to the Isaak Walton Killam Hospital Poison Center to ascertain the symptoms of slow, chronic carbon monoxide poisoning, we were convinced (wanted to be convinced) that this was what had happened to me.

In the end, we knew it was not poison. As much as we wished, it was not. It was MS after all, and it was MS that put me in the hospital. And in the middle of the night, one night of that very long week in November 1996, the hospital became a very frantic place. Medical staff were called over the sound system to a station muster. Clearly there was an emergency, as the announcements continued for a time and there was obvious, hustling activity in the halls. An accident, no doubt. The trauma team called. The heat on the ward was stifling. My head was sweating, my hair soggy. I couldn't stand the plastic cover underneath my pillowcase—so hot, so very hot. I whipped it off. I'd confess later. I had been rudely awoken, and in the heat I was carried off to a warm adventure. I was in Nassau. There, the heat was delicious.

Trade Winds

Nassau, Bahamas. Dr. Theo Hills and I had been rejected by the government official as being dressed too casually (that is, wearing walking shorts) to attend the meeting with the Minister of Tourism. We would have to change. In the elevator on the way back to our rooms, Theo looked a tad disgruntled. "Do you really feel like getting dressed up?" he asked. "No." I replied. "Let's go into town. You were looking for a bookstore. I know an excellent one."

"Perfect." Conferences are best when there are unexpected turns. Conferences about Small Islands held on small islands are grand that way.

Nassau in May is delightful. Blossoming and fragrant. The light is bright but not harsh. The air is sweet as the trade winds blow. Since we missed the meeting due to a swim in the blue-green sea and the inadvertent dress-protocol misconduct, enjoying the city seemed the logical next choice. Dr. Hills, an anthropologist with an esteemed career in Caribbean study spanning decades, shared generously his superb knowledge of indigenous literature and advised me on the best writing. With purchases in hand, we next went for ice cream. I'll always remember that treat, purchased at a little ice-cream parlour next to the Hotel Colonial. The smiley-eyed clerk scooped me a huge cone—raspberry crème fondue. It was so luscious, cool, and tangy. I love raspberries. We took a circuitous, sight-seeing bus route back to the Nassau Beach Hotel and rejoined conference activities.

That night there was a display of Caribbean culture in the hotel's patio garden on the beach, with music, dancing, and food. I called a premature end to my evening, even though it was the last night of the conference. I simply decided that was enough. My legs were done in. I had not missed anything else, attended all sessions, delivered my paper, visited, and seen the sights. Next day I had an early meeting to attend. My roommate had returned early as well. She, too, was tired in body and legs. It didn't cross my mind there was anything untoward. Then I got home.

The whole family was on hand for a traditional Victoria Day weekend planting of the garden. I was feeling tawny from the Bahamas, which was an excellent way to face the long weekend, as it was usually prime time for a burn. I imagined I was protected. I already felt like summer, so it felt good to be out in the heat, working the good red earth. It would be the last garden I planted with full strength in my legs.

In the days ahead, gradually and repeatedly, I was bumping into walls, doorways, and people. My left foot dragged. The toes of my shoes got scuffed going upstairs, and the heels scuffed on the way down. I couldn't walk when I first stood up. A sensation that my right leg was full of mercury—liquid and heavy—pinned me to the floor. I had no choice but to allow it to complete its course from hip to toes before I could lift my right leg and move.

I remembered what the doctor said a year-and-a-half before, "It could be MS. But since there is no cure and no treatment, it is not something to worry about now. Track your symptoms for a year-and-a-half so that, then, a clinical diagnosis can be made."

Oh, I had been tracking the symptoms, all right. I felt a pang of concern when I attempted to resume running mid-winter, and, day by day, I experienced a growing unwillingness in my legs to move forward, until acceleration became so difficult that I switched to the aerobics class and continued with that until balance was a problem. "Must be my bad leg acting up again," I decided, and took to rowing, stairs, and lifting weights. Then one day I was pinned under the leg press. Legs with no strength. I knew why.

It was time to tell Dr. Flanagan. My appointment occurred on a classic early June day on the Island. Greens enough for every need, lilacs in bloom everywhere, and lady's slipper in the woods. This seemed to matter to me.

When she walked in the examining room I said, "Well, Barb, I have MS." She sat on the stool. She agreed. We talked about it there, straightforwardly, as though it was routine, not monumental. A glitch? MS is unpredictable by nature, and perhaps it would amount to very little. That was the bright side. We didn't consider any other side. By the time I got home from work that day, I had decided one can choose on which side to live. I clearly knew which side I preferred, and with a family it was unjust to choose any but that. Just now.

I walked into the unknown with that embossed on my heart.

The Broom Closet Conference

June lolled along, more lush and more green each day, as if every winter expectation had been granted with verdant generosity. It felt a bit like a dream here, where everything is beautiful every day, the air so sweet and clean. What I had to say didn't match, somehow. Yet I knew I must tell them, my co-workers Laurie Brinklow and Anna MacDonald. They are my friends, too. They should know. They could help me. It would come as a shot out of the blue . . . the green. But the day had arrived. It could not go on otherwise because it was getting hard to manage. I was amazed how many people I had bumped into who apologized to me before I had a chance to apologize to them. (Michael says it is because people are so naturally kind that they are willing to accept responsibility for the bumping, no matter its source. Why does that comfort me?) The task faced me, in spite of all the greenness and kindness. The task of telling. I couldn't wait for a gray day, could I?

Well, I had it all thought through in my mind. There was no other choice, really. We couldn't meet in the Board Room, as there was constant traffic there. We couldn't go outdoors since that meant the blasted stairs and chances were I might make a spectacle of myself. That left the broom closet. I practiced it in my head all the way driving in to town that morning. I would just blurt it out, start to finish, before they got a chance to say anything. This would not be a brainstorming conference, or a sharing anything conference. It would be a short delivery-of-data conference, then it would end. It is all I could do for a start. Later, we would talk, after lunch, under a tree, outdoors. I'd have some reserve then.

"I want to talk to you in the broom closet." Anna and Laurie followed me down the hall. Our offices were in a row, from the east end of Dalton Hall, west to the staircase. The broom closet was on the far side of the staircase. It was spacious and, as always, tidy, the way Margie liked it. It was not where we usually met to discuss things. In fact I had never before suggested it as a meeting room.

"This is odd, I know, but I have to speak to you in confidence because I need your help. Please understand that I do not mean you to be upset." They nodded. I kept on track. [. . . nerve . . . nerve, I need nerve . . .]

"It's an out-of-the-ordinary thing to say, so I will just come out and say it. I have MS." They were stock still. "The fact is, it isn't anything to worry about, not in the usual way, because it is such an eccentric disease. I'll be fine, but right now I need your help, and I am not ready for the world to know this of me yet. Peter and Harry should not know. They fret. In time I'll tell them, too, but not now."

You should know why Peter and Harry would fret. Harry Baglole was the Director of the Institute of Island Studies (IIS), at UPEI, where I worked. Dr. Peter Meincke, a physics professor, was my close associate in the development and management of the Small Islands Information Network, affectionately known as "the SIIN"—a computer network designed to keep people who do work on small islands, all around the world, in communication with each other. We designed it. The Institute did an extraordinary amount of work with this small team. We were it. We were friends, and we worked well together. As a team we lent new meaning to the word "productive." More than once an international associate, knowing what we did, assumed the whole of Dalton Hall was taken up by the IIS and was then amazed to learn we occupy one half of one floor. We cared about each other. That was why we were in the broom closet.

The color drained from Laurie's and Anna's faces . . . just what I wanted to avoid but knew was inevitable. We shared some hugs. [. . . I know what I've got to say—keep on track . . . !] "You see, at the moment I am having some difficulty walking. My feet drag, my stamina is poor, my balance is off, and, when I stand up, it takes about thirty seconds before a heavy liquid feeling makes its way down my right leg, releasing me to walk. You can see this makes it tricky to run down the hall to answer a phone." Our phone system was very basic. We each had a phone in our office with our own phone number. When somebody was out of his or her office, one of us would run like a gazelle to pick up the ringing phone. [. . . steady! . . . I was nearly finished . . . .] "Also it is hard for me to make trips across campus through the day. I am fine if I stay put, but going up and down four flights of stairs and across the campus repeatedly as well is a bit more than I can manage." [. . . . hot in here . . .]

Instantly, they understood, I could see they got it. Whew! For now, the trekking tasks would bypass me, and this discreetly. I was sure this siege would end soon. Not soon enough, indeed, not soon enough.

It was the only time I have ever held a conference in a broom closet, and so the memory of it is special to me. This is where my adventure really began, for now I was in it real and earnest.

June had come and gone in its usual, luscious way. Like a feasting, glamorous dragonfly after a cold, barren winter, June on our Island awakens to gorge in outrageous beauty. It is on the edge of being too much.

I was thinking, as we looked to summer, one day from July, that one can cope with most anything if one can devise a management system that is creative and effective. MS is a management problem. Usually.

The Ballerina Cast and the Bus

Meet Michael at the Queen Elizabeth Hospital where Dr. Profit has been called in to see to the injury . . ." I hung up the phone, left my office, and headed for the hospital.

A ruptured Achilles tendon. Michael had a cast that kept his toe pointed like a ballet dancer's, in order for the frayed tendon to meet and mend back together. This and crutches for the entire summer. You can't sport a walking cast with a pointed toe! Poor Michael. The thought of such an injury makes me shiver. How it must hurt! It was the last day of school for teachers, days after the students had gone on vacation. There was a pick-up game of basketball and rip! ouch! There it was—a severed Achilles tendon. It sounded absolutely terrible. It is a true fact that summer comes not a minute too soon for teachers. Not an indulgence, but an essential time of renewal. I could only imagine what disappointment accompanied this injury.

I knew I would have to buck up. I thought I could do just fine, myself, but all of a sudden I recognized that I depended on Michael as a support system for me. Now I was to be the support system for him. Now I would see what I was made of.

Things were busy at work. Too much work for the too few of us, which was about normal. At home there was much to do now that everything grew wildly. Grass, flowers, vegetables, weeds. Michael mastered his crutches, but what a bother they were to him. Imagine not being able to carry anything because both hands are taken up with crutches. He said the ankle did not hurt, though, so that was something. I knew I had overdone it trying to make my darling comfortable, as much as I could. I was bushed. Maybe this was good training for me. I was curious to know what my limits were.

Perhaps it was all the doing, but I became more and more wobbly—not a surprise, more an expectation—so at last I had to say something to Harry and Peter. Laurie and Anna insisted on the importance of this. We sat in Laurie's office with Harry and Peter, coffee perking. It felt like a family meeting. I found this more difficult than meeting in the broom closet. The solemn looks on their faces, the seriousness of it, the finality of admitting to the reality. It won't go away. This is IT. Forever. And their concern. I did not want to worry them, but such news would anyway. The next day Harry brought me a beautiful ebony walking stick which he got in Kenya. "If you need a stick, you might as well go in style!" To me it is a treasure, a piece of art, not just a stick.

Ten days later my brother Tom and his wife Lissa were hit by a bus just outside Lunenburg. I spoke to Tom, who was in Lunenburg Hospital. His greatest fear was for Lissa who was in the Victoria General Hospital, not expected to live, and he could not get to her. So the next day I went to Halifax, and for the first time in my life, I found myself in Neurological ICU—not for myself, but for Lissa. I was terrified for my sister-in-law. She did not look much like somebody who would live. She lay on the striker bed, traveling back and forth, back and forth with tubes from everywhere, including her brain, connected to all manner of machine. Her head was enlarged, hair matted with blood. I can still see her there, though I do not wish to remember. I put my hand on her hand. The nurse said that it might excite her and affect her heartbeat. I removed it.

I went to Lunenburg to see Tom. He hurt so much I could only hug him softly. He would be okay. His head was fine again, and his legs and broken ribs would get better. He was alive.

The next morning I made my way to the MS Clinic with my ebony walking stick. I was afraid that if I got stuck in the middle of Robie Street without a stick to warn people I was in difficulty, they might be tempted to honk the horn and keep on driving. There was no Clinic because of summer vacation, but Pauline Weldon was in her office in the basement of Camp Hill Hospital. I hunted around the hospital and was completely worn out by the time I found her. She saw instantly that I was in trouble and offered me a chair. I told her my name, that I was recently diagnosed with MS, that my brother and sister-in-law had gotten hit by a bus, that he was okay in Lunenburg Hospital, but that she was in Victoria General and might die, and I burst into a torrent of tears. And that was how I met Pauline. She listened and offered some advice, which when I got home I was to follow, and she made an appointment for me to see Dr. Jock Murray in September.

Back at the hospital I sat beside Lissa, my hand cupping hers with my arm traveling up and down with the striker bed. Sometimes you have to take things into your own hands (literally!). I could understand that her heart would be confused if I was tickling her hand, causing fluctuations in heartbeat. But I also knew that her heart would break if she thought she was alone . . . all alone . . . nobody to love her back. With my hand over hers, she might know someone who loved her was there. I couldn't take the chance of leaving her alone. The nurses seemed to understand because they did not say a word. Hours passed like this.

In the hospital elevator, a young orderly spied my walking stick, the one Harry gave me the morning after we had that meeting about my MS. "Awesome walking stick!"

"Yes," I answered, "awesome."

"Is it a fertility symbol?"

"No, no, just a carving!" But it was not just a carving. It was ebony, with a snake curling all around, and a woman's head carved there. Whose head? I had only recently myself been to Kenya. I had stood at the top of the Ngong Hills and looked down, with philodendron curling wildly about my feet. (I wondered if my Kenyan friends would think it strange that we put these plants in pots and feed them special food.) Because I had been there, where everyone smiles in spite of everything, a simple ebony stick was more to me, a sculpture from Eden. In that moment when I needed a stick, I grasped my sculpture.

Several days passed. Tom cajoled his way out of Lunenburg Hospital. I was sitting by Lissa's bed when he arrived at the Victoria General. Blessedly she was out of the striker bed. Tom had a cane and was bent over and in much pain. But the pain in his heart for Lissa was worse than that he carried in his body. He wore it on his face. It is another picture I shall never forget.

Tom sang, read, and talked to Lissa, and she woke from the coma. The Psalm for that August day she awoke was Psalm 139, which is, by coincidence, also among the Prayers to be Used at Sea, fitting for Captain Tom. It was a beginning.

O Lord, thou has searched me out and known me:
thou knowest my path . . .

Whither shall I go then from thy spirit?:
or wither shall I flee from thy presence?
If I climb up into heaven, thou art there:
if I go down to hell thou art there also,
If I take the wings of the morning,
and dwell in the uttermost parts of the sea,
Even there also shall thy hand lead me,
and thy right hand shall hold me.

Even the days that were planned for me,
when as yet there was none of them!
> *If I count them, they are more in number than the sand:*
> *when I wake up, I am present with thee.*

We wept.

That summer was spent praying for Lissa. Tom had his cane. Michael had his cast and his crutches. I had my walking stick. Tom said he could only think of the first day back at school and the requisite composition "What I Did on My Summer Vacation" and the drawing of us that would accompany the story. We did chuckle, in spite of it all.

Michael put a plastic bag over his cast, and the garden had no weeds and perfect edging. I went to the hospital for Solu-Medrol, crawling in, bouncing out. It seemed like a miracle. Tom said he learned about love, that it was a gift. And thus passed the summer. I found out what we were made of, in spades.

In my notebook I recorded, "Mid-July Blossom Count." It read:

Today's blossom count: valerian, cleome, snapdragon, dahlia, golden yarrow, anise hyssop, catnip, oregano, lavender, bergamot, sweet William, purple lythrum, painted daisy, candytuft, bell flower, astilbe, roses (pink, red, and peace), rudbeckias, cosmos, potentilla (yellow and pink), clematis, veronica, spiderwort, Cupid's dart, zinnia, marigold, carnation poppy, petunia, geranium, lavatera, baby's breath, delphinium. In a basket for the dining room table—a bouquet of spirea, white yarrow, mallow, and St. John's wort.

There must be a reason I make blossom counts. I think it is because I see this as a "glad count," and it makes up for the mental counts I make of the other sort. Hands today? Feet? Leg? Can I say linen? You can talk if you can say linen.

At last there are some nasturtiums blooming. I gave up hope two weeks ago and added some dwarf marigolds to the front window-boxes, dressed the east side (garden side) boxes (leaving the nasturtiums in where feasible) with salmon geraniums, dwarf marigolds, white petunias, mixed trailing lobelia, purple alyssum, and some rosy impatiens. The west side I left alone. Now it blossoms.

We had a lovely supper outside this evening. Cecily and Mille set the picnic table with candles and linen and a bouquet of golden yarrow, veronica, Lythrum, and candytuft. And there were new peas cooked with mint, barbecued parsnips, curried rice salad, tomato-oregano pork chops, and whipped turnip with nutmeg. Over supper we had some discussion about "high summer" versus "deep summer." I say "high" since "deep" must mean under snow. Michael says high summer is June 21. Deep summer is now. He says "deep" is what they say in *The Wind and the Willows*, so I can't argue. (Or, I can't remember, so I concede.) Deep summer it is!! Hot, anyway! Despite the heat, I cannot bring myself to get an air conditioner. Michael thinks it might make things more comfortable for me in our bedroom, but I hate the thought of air-conditioned air, and, besides, which window would I give up? I like it in my Treehouse with five windows, on three sides, all opened and blowing in the sweet smells of summer. We wait so long to get them I cannot bear to snuff their perfume away. Perhaps, one day it will come to that, but not this day!

Michael got a new cast and this one straightens his foot a little but not enough to be without the crutches.

Note: Next summer I want lots of lavender. I made lavender ice cream and lavender cookies, which we ate on a very hot day sitting under the shade of the maple tree, and this was yummy. We shouldn't run out of lavender blossoms. And I need some for the linen chest. Also, I need more basil and more nasturtium. And I did not like the window-boxes this year—too much yellow and gold . . . need red, blue, pink.

The Appointment

My very first appointment at the Dalhousie MS Research Unit was on a perfectly wonderful day in September. Michael was with me for moral support and a comforting presence. Our neighbors and friends, Dr. Elizabeth Townsend and Dr. Harry Robertson, told us that I could not do better than Jock Murray, for whom they had the highest regard. The finest of neurologists, they said. I trust Liz and Harry. They are adopted family and colleagues of Dr. Murray's at Dalhousie University, where Harry is head of Neuropharmacology and Liz is head of Occupational Therapy. These are impeccable references. I considered it a blessing that I could get to see him. God bless Pauline Weldon.

Funny, how clearly I remember the day, how beautiful it was. I so love the soft, fragrant days of September when the sun is heather gold and the air shimmers. The MS Clinic was then in the old Camp Hill Hospital, which was destined for demolition and was on its last legs. I knew I was another in what must be a tiring day of appointments for MS sufferers, one after another after another. (We've got to find another word—patients? No. People? Obviously. Patience? Certainly. MSers? Who are we?) I was inclined to see myself on the more hopeful side of the disease, at this point, except for the tiny misgivings in the far corners of my mind because of the certain knowledge of all the experts who wrote all the books, which, fortunately or unfortunately, I had read. I guessed there could be more trouble.

By the time September rolled around, I was sure this appointment was a good idea. Enough had happened to unnerve me, and I needed to get to the bottom of a few things. I can't remember what I thought would happen, but having grown up in a medical family, the presence of a good doctor was a reassuring, nonthreatening, thing. Doctors do not make me nervous. My father was a brilliant diagnostician. They used to fly him places so he could assist with puzzling cases. He had schooled us to view a physician's best diagnostic tool as the wisdom a patient had about his or her own body. I hoped I could remember the important things, though at this point I was not too sure what was important. I would use my instinct for now. I was glad Michael was with me so we could learn together what the future might hold. I had on yellow, a jaundice-yellow hospital gown. How vain of me not to like the color!

Dr. Murray came in, greeted us with a firm handshake and the clear eye contact of a secure person. This engendered confidence in me. Dr. Murray bears some interesting resemblances to my father—the stature, the good posture, the trim build, about five-foot-ten. It is very handy to have some perfect stranger whom you must learn to trust bear resemblance to the one you trusted most. I was sitting on the examining table taking visual notes. Dr. Murray had thick, wavy hair, once dark, now turning salt and pepper. My father had this hair (I did not inherit the curls . . .) as did all his brothers. Baldness was not a Gallant male concern—rather, very thick, wavy, dark hair to the end. I thought of this as Acadian hair since it seemed to be the family rule, except for my grandfather's fair, straight hair, which I inherited. But Dr. Murray is Scottish. (There is one thing I have never understood about my father's family: Why does a family whose mother tongue is French speak English with a lilting Gaelic accent? Wherever did that come from? Must be the hair!)

Dr. Murray wore his lab coat (the kind Daddy passed on to us for costumes), a striped shirt with a white collar, and a gorgeous tie. I like beautiful ties, so I noticed that. All in all, it made a very handsome picture.

He spoke to us as the intelligent, compassionate, interested physician Harry and Liz had said he was. He had a good voice—calm, stalwart, with the erudite accent of a literate person, an accent that travels well anywhere on the globe. I guess one calls that a mid-Atlantic accent. He was relaxed and personable. Clearly, he liked people. You could see that. He said, "Who diagnosed you?" I said, "I did." He said, "You're right." Later, at the end of the appointment he added, "It is benign MS, a non-degenerative form of the disease." Benign. A tiny little word with enormous relief attached. Non-degenerative. No wheelchair, I thought. It was good enough for now.

There was a lot to absorb, much to ask. One couldn't quite know yet, this early on, what all the questions were. It contained an edge of the impossible I could not identify just then. It is a good thing Jock Murray was such a man, otherwise I would have thought the best idea might be to forget the whole bloody thing. Go away and forget about it. Come what may. And then we discovered the marvellous thing about the good doctor. He was an unflinching, unabashed, committed optimist even though, better than anyone, he knew the real truth! This was the doctor for me. Michael and I left feeling very satisfied, and my husband said to me—I think there was relief in his voice—"You are in good hands." He knew I would never return if the doctor was inclined to glumness.

From the MS Clinic we went to the hospital to see Lissa. She was out of ICU and in a room now, and could say a few words. She recognized me and said, haltingly "I-am-so-worried about you." News of my having MS was one of the last things that she learned before the accident, and this was the first indication that she was connected to her past. And, finally, she had remembered that the good-looking man who came to see her every day was her husband. This too, was enough for now.

Later that month, the Institute of Island Studies held an international conference, which I walked into feeling terrific and walked out of with numb feet. It had been an exhausting job, this conference, but interesting and a success. As we packed boxes of materials to be moved from Shaw's at Brackley Beach back to the office, I felt my feet get numb. It grew quickly worse, extending up my legs to my thighs like iron boots. And I became encased in a very tight girdle. This dramatic change took only three days. Walking became very difficult and painful, and it hurt to stand. My skin was so hypersensitive that a soft sweatsuit felt like sandpaper. The condition continued to grow worse, and another dose of Solu-Medrol was advised. This time the symptoms that receded first were the worst, then slowly over the ensuing month, the rest faded. I appeared to be in pretty good shape, as my mobility was not visibly affected. My walking looked quite normal, but I was in considerable discomfort and concentrated carefully. The numbness never did completely disappear in my feet and the tingliness remained quite apparent on walks.

Benign. He said benign.

Words/Tenebrae

It was May. Late May and my first extraordinary event. Peter and Donna Meincke brought me a collection of books-on-tape to fill the gap because my vision was too blurry to read. How I enjoyed the books.

I missed being at work. I kept the windows open to let in the fragrances of May—first lilacs, tilled soil, and such—since I was living in the Treehouse. But I hadn't figured out how to answer the phone. First there was the problem of getting the headpiece off the cradle, which was a real dilemma since my hands wouldn't cooperate with much of anything and certainly not a slender phone. I'd pick up the entire phone, tip it upside down and scoop the headpiece up from the bed and hope the caller was still there so I could say "hello." Saying hello was the hardest. That is a darned difficult word, almost as bad as linen. I wanted to say "yes!" but it just wasn't me. I never said "yes!" when I answered the phone. Too self-conscious. But, saying hello, I know I sounded as if something was wrong. Drunk.

I had a beastly slur. I could not have imagined that there is such a string of events that must come into play in order for words to be delivered properly formed. It is not something one considers when speech is no trial. I found this the greatest humiliation. Greater than all the rest. That this ability had deteriorated to the point that I was unhappily self-conscious with speaking was frustrating in the extreme. I was baffled, stymied, disconcerted. This really was horrible. Michael tried to put a positive spin on it, saying that if I sounded like a drunk, I was an amiable drunk. The problem of the phone persisted, as during the day I was the only one home, and there were several things in the offing that needed tending.

When the producer from Morningside called, I was unnerved, yet there was no way to flee. Could I go to the Charlottetown CBC studio for a discussion about a tax reform that would give stay-at-home mothers childcare benefits in line with those of working mothers? Near to my heart, this.

I could not go. I could not talk. I could not drive. I could not walk. It was obvious I could not talk. On the radio you want people who can talk. I proposed she (the producer) call Beverly Smith in Calgary. Beverly would be excellent. And I apologized for my incapacity and without thinking about the repercussions I dared to say I had MS and was having a rough time just then. And since that day I never heard another word from Morningside. Even though three weeks later I could speak just fine. It never got as bad as that again.

We got another style of telephone with a headpiece, which is easy to pick up. Beverly was wonderful, and I wrote to tell her so. But I didn't write any more letters to Morningside. There didn't seem any point since, clearly, they had no further use for me.

I felt no grudge. It was a family misunderstanding. I loved Peter Gzowski like an old friend. He was my daily companion through the *This Country in the Morning* and *Morningside* years. He was present as I reared a family. In the evenings, Michael would say, "What was Peter up to today?" I hold the CBC in my affection because it binds a national family together in a country that makes no sense. Canada is too vast, too diverse to make sense unless we recognize the reason for it to be is love: an effort of love is what wills its existence. More than the national ledger, it is this will that makes Canada. The CBC is a safe environment for the Canadian family to share its hopes and dreams, its struggles and triumphs.

One year when we were perched between the last bitter, tired days of winter and the expectant hope of spring, a particular sharing was taking place across the land. Bill Richardson, the then host of *RSVP*, read a letter that touched him so, he wondered what the rest of us were feeling. The letter was about a turning point in the life of one ordinary, remarkable Canadian. Were there other turning points in other lives? "Please write to me." And we did. Writing is how families stay connected. I wrote, too. This is what Bill read:

Turning Point/Tenebrae

It is Maundy Thursday. This evening—the Seder, then Tenebrae. Tenebrae . . . darkness, shadow. Out of the darkness—light—my turning point.

> *I will give thee the treasures of darkness*
> *and the hidden riches of secret places."*
>
> (Isaiah 45:3)

It must be true that life is never quite what it seems, or at least quite what we expect it to be. Certainly not what we demand it to be. The changes and chances of life are most extraordinary when I look at them from the outside, watching.

Several years ago I was diagnosed with MS. This was not much fun. Frankly, I didn't like this at all. Before, everything was easy. Hands that worked, feet that ran fast, indefatigable energy. Such a fine feeling to be able to accomplish everything! And now? Slow. I am slow. My hands are not the good friends they used to be, my feet have lost their wings, I am weary. How strange, how very strange. Is this me? It feels like I am on the outside, watching.

There were some moments of sadness, surely a mourning for my lost, vibrant, good health. And yet, that recognized, the depression promised me in all those books never came. I am surrounded by loved ones who clearly see beyond this weariness. It doesn't seem to matter. Not to them for sure, but I want to be a good wife, a helpful mother, and one day to walk in the hemlock forest with grandchildren. Will I always walk in the hemlocks? Where was that depression, and why did it not come?

When everything was simple, accomplishments flew by unnoticed. Now my days are filled with endless, small triumphs. Everything is a triumph. How remarkable I am! When I walk I must think about it, but I have thought so well that I doubt you would notice how hard I am thinking. The garden is as productive as ever and as beautiful. I made my youngest son that dreamed-of duffle coat . . . heavy. It was so heavy I could just barely handle it. But how handsome it is. There is bread rising. I have a beautiful ebony walking stick.

Then Tenebrae came, and I knelt there in the darkness, wondering. In the darkness everything seemed clear, touchable. I felt the treasure in that darkness—the sweet, secret treasure. And I knew in that moment why I am still so glad about life . . . it is not my body, but my soul that is being made fit. The turning point . . . from darkness to light. Now, from the inside, knowing.

> *Yet even in the darkness is no darkness with thee,*
> *but the night is as clear as the day*
> *the darkness and the light to thee are both alike.*
>
> (Psalm 139:11)

Tonight, I will kneel in the darkness of Tenebrae, the shadow, as we sing Gregorio Allegri's *Miserere Mei* and I will know, again, the truth. *Deo gratias.*

Counted Steps

Last night, first frost
hearty thanks for the rest
of the past night,
the gift of a new day.

Four hundred thirty-six
steps to the mailbox
counted carefully
to conquer the fearful distance.

A bouquet must wait, but
later, there will be more steps.
Marigold, mums, Michaelmas daisy,
sage, verbena, phlox will
take their place in a posy,
to turn round and round.

There is always a best side. In everything.

5 ❧ COUNTED STEPS
New York, New York

Itook a stroll just now, around the garden and down to the river.
Soon it will be time to clean up the garden for winter. Yesterday
I harvested the onions and set them to dry in the barn loft. The
crown-of-thorn ornamental squash I planted as an experiment are
very beautiful. That's good, since they take up plenty of room, and—
just imagine—a big plant that is not even edible, in a vegetable garden
. . . purely to have something beautiful to look at. In the end the family will all think these very beautiful, and nobody will wonder about
the space they took. Last year this time, Cecily and I were preparing
for the Big Yard Sale.

I don't particularly like yard sales, but Cecily and I had a purpose.
We were raising money for an adventure. It was the end of August
when she said, "Mama, I want to go to New York City, and I want you
to come with me. We will have a great time!" Of all the places in the
world I want yet to see, New York is not in the top ten. In any case it
seemed very big and completely out-of-scale for my stamina and my
legs. I was thinking about those adorable little New England villages,
but Cecily had another idea. She worked very hard to convince me it
would be great—the opera, the museums, Central Park—and that if I
paced myself it would be no problem at all. I tried hard to deduce the
importance of this journey to her, and the possible better suitability
of a friend her age as a travel companion. In the end I saw clearly it
was a moment not to miss, that my daughter had chosen her mother
as the ideal travel companion—no matter what—and I knew in my
heart any risk was worth this compliment. Thus, in September, the
Big Yard Sale.

We were very organized. We had things set up in the middle bay
of the barn with spill-out to the yard in front, so that we could carry
on, no matter the weather. There were tables for collectibles, dishes
and doo-dads, bookshelves full of books. There were sweaters, jeans, a
clothes rack hung with freshly washed and ironed clothes. Cecily said

she doubted normal people did this for a yard sale, but I insisted nobody would buy anything that was not in good condition. However, I discovered clothes, in a very limited size range, are not big sellers. There was some old furniture, toys, sports equipment, a costume basket, a water pump, and a few tools. We served fresh, hot coffee, and cookies, right out of the oven. It is amazing how many people come to a yard sale. We made enough money to pay for my airline ticket, which was our goal.

A trip to the library netted a huge armload of books about New York City and Cecily bought a copy of *Fodor's New York*, which included a big, pull-out map. Of all the books, I particularly liked Michele Landsberg's *"This Is New York, Honey!" A Homage to Manhattan, with Love and Rage*. After reading this, I felt I really knew the city, and I was anxious to get there. And by the time we boarded the plane, we had all but memorized the map. We also knew, from *Fodor's*, that if ever I needed a wheelchair, they would be easy to find in most places.

Jane Swan met us at the airport. We were staying with Jane. I had been her babysitter. When she was ten months old she tried to climb the Christmas tree, which was not a great idea and it came crashing down. Jane crept happily along from underneath the branches, completely unscathed, though the tree was demolished. I had many adventures with little Jane. She grew into an amazing woman. New York greeted us as a stunning silhouette against a brilliant autumn sunset, which all but took our breath away. We tucked into Jane's cozy apartment in the Upper East Side, a stone's throw from Museum Mile and Central Park. Amazing! In the midst of everything! How exciting. I had reserved a wheelchair for Toronto. I did not use it. I had reserved a wheelchair for La Guardia. I did not use it. I was feeling pretty smart. I have come to understand that Cecily can convince anybody to achieve anything. It is something about the way she says, "You can do it!" that makes one a believer.

So, there we were in this immense city, puny-legged me and the Big Apple. It was a little overwhelming, but exciting all the same, so I was glad of the adventure.

We had a glorious time at the Metropolitan Museum of Art, which turned out to be much bigger than one could ever anticipate.

We took a whole day making our way through only a portion of the European section! Sess would wander off when I needed a rest. Sitting on a bench I studied a triptych, or a Botticelli, Renoir, Monet, or Picasso—one could hardly complain. She'd come back, "Come on, Mom. You have to see this!" and she'd thread the way through a maze of galleries till we stood in front of some remarkable creation. We had a yummy, healthy lunch, finishing with an indulgent chocolate delicacy. The Metropolitan Museum's restaurant is in the dining-room that had been the site of the fountain in the children's book, *From the Mixed-Up Files of Mrs. Basil E. Frankweiler*. We had promised Gethin we would take a photo, but the fountain was no more, though the ceiling fixtures were the same. I felt all-round indulged. I might have taken a wheelchair, but the museum looked very innocent upon entering, and I only saw one wheelchair all day and never did see where the museum kept its supply. And, besides, I was just fine, enjoying being on foot like everyone else. It made me feel the same as everyone else.

We learned the bus system and how great it was for getting a good view of the city. The buses travel slowly, so it is possible to see the change from neighborhood to neighborhood. We walked lots of places, made our way to the top of the Empire State Building, and had lunch at Macy's—a must, so we were told. We took power-breaks for tea or coffee, which did the trick for me. We went to the Metropolitan Opera, where we saw Franco Zeffirelli's production of *Turandot*. It was a feast for the eyes as well as the ears. Zeffirelli and the substantial budget of the Met came together in opulent, exquisite extravagance with this production. During the first intermission, Jane and I went for opera glasses because I could not believe the size of Jane Eglan and had to see her up close. A great big Turandot. For me, it didn't work because I couldn't believe the rather fit, trim Calaf would fall for her instead of the beautiful, faithful Liú. But I got my dream of hearing "Nessun dorma" sung at the Met. I learned a good lesson that most anything, even a "big" thing like lasting through an opera, can be managed. I did not drink a drop of liquid after four o'clock, purposefully dehydrating, as I was not sure how I would fare with the loo, and I put my legs up for a rest before dinner to recharge stamina.

Then, my big triumph. On Saturday, with Jane home from work, we had plans to have a picnic breakfast in Central Park. It was pouring rain, so we decided to eat "somewhere" instead of the picnic, and we three set out in the rain. It was lovely in the park. We had an umbrella and rain jackets. There were not very many people about, which seemed a shame to me as it was a fine morning. I suppose the people we did see thought our little trio rather peculiar, sitting on a park bench in the rain, just talking. They didn't know I was refueling. In the end, Jane figured we walked about two miles in the park. We started on the East Side, went right across and up through the park, passed the Dakota and on up Columbus Avenue until we found an oyster bar for lunch. I did that! I walked all that way. From there we visited the Cathedral of St. John the Divine, and then had a hair-raising taxi ride to Times Square. I think it is compulsory, this mad taxi ride, but blessedly the other rides were very uneventful, by comparison. I was making a special trip to a tobacconist on 5th Avenue, but he had accidentally sold the last can of Rattray's Red Raparee I had called about and reserved. I was very disappointed because it was to be a gift for a dear friend. The towering, big, smiley tobacconist felt badly and gave me a very fine wooden cigar box, which I took home and turned into a decoupaged memory box of our trip to New York and gave to Cecily for Christmas.

All these things I did, which proved to me most anything is possible, for I had thought this impossible. We found everybody in New York so helpful, polite, and kind. People couldn't have been nicer to us. After the trip, an idea fermented . . . an invention for people like me who need a bit more leg staying-power. Not a whole lot, but a little more to allow one to keep up with the adventure. I'm working on it. I call it the "Leg Saver," a collapsable, very light device for pushing someone in, yet compact enough to carry on one's back with a strap. It would not be for everyone, obviously, because it requires a buddy to do the pushing. It would be perfect for persons of modest weight, who can walk but need to rest at times. All I need is an engineer to work with me on the design, plus a pocketful of money to create a prototype and begin production. I know there are many like me who cannot go the distance, but who are not ready for a wheelchair.

Getting home was the trickiest part, for after all the comings and goings in the Big Apple, it was little Caribou, Nova Scotia, which nearly did me in. I was traveling alone, as Cecily stayed with Jane for a few more days before continuing on to Toronto and Montreal. I took the bus from Halifax to New Glasgow, and a taxi from New Glasgow to the ferry. This is the fastest and cheapest way to get home. I would get the four o'clock ferry, and Michael would meet me on the other side. That was the plan. The ferry arrived (from Wood Islands) in heavy rain and even heavier winds. But instead of heading off again at four o'clock, it tied up for the day. That was it—too windy to sail again. Well, great. Marooned in a wind storm. I went down to the porter's office where the taxi had dropped off my suitcase. Here I discovered: 1) no ferry crew would be driving to the Island via the bridge; 2) nor were any passengers heading back to the Island; 3) the ferry terminal was now closed. Nasty turn of events.

I'd never stayed in a ferry bunkhouse before, but I was grateful, very grateful, to be taken in. I was to help myself to anything in the fridge. Joyce, my roommate and host, went back to finish her shift on the boat. I took an apple and went to bed to read. It didn't really matter if I slept, since I only wanted to get home on the first boat in the morning. Surely it would go. It poured and blew all night. It is difficult to breathe when you are not used to a place completely bathed in cigarette smoke.

The first boat did go at seven, and I was on it! Dear Joyce insisted on giving me breakfast onboard and then found me a drive, since I was marooned again. The ferry would arrive at Wood Islands at 8:30 or so, depending on the wind, so Michael would be long at school. Thus, I climbed (truly!) up to my seat, along with a suitcase and a shopping bag from the Metropolitan Museum of Art, into the cab of a twenty-two wheeler and rode to Belfast School. Quite a view way up there! I had often teased Michael with the idea of going to Pro-Train to become a truck driver and then going all over the country in one of those trucks with the sleeping cab. No more such thoughts. Besides, I was really only interested in the cab. The huge truck pulled over on the shoulder, not the usual vehicle to pull up in front of the school. I climbed out safely. Danny helped with my bags. Danny was the driver. It was an ususal trip from the ferry. Danny assured me his seat was much more comfortable than the one for the passenger, which had no springs. Thank goodness for him.

I had my keys, so I took the car and went home. All of a sudden, it all seemed so spacious—home I mean—after an apartment in the city and the density of Manhattan. I looked out window after window to see the familiar landscape of Pearsie, now in late fall, and went out to feel the air and smell autumn.

New York is one thing. Home is another.

The Rant

This stupid damn disease. It never gives up. Relentlessly, on and on it goes. I don't think anybody can be expected to understand what it feels like inside when outside looks normal. Fine. Healthy. There isn't anything one can say when told, "You look great!" Amusing when people say, "You're looking better now . . . " when I am feeling worse. (Actually, it is good in some ways because who would like to look wan and sickly?) My outside looks are a bit of tomfoolery because inside is weary (oh! the fatigue that is ever there), weak (I thought I could do that, but no), unnerved (now that's just great, the legs have given up so how do I get back to where I started?), or worried (whatever will happen next, and when?).

I lost sensation in my hands, then, after waiting seven months, I gave up waiting to get my hands back. Instead I have accepted my peculiar hands as the status quo. I can do a button, even a small button, when I am watching closely, but my hands do not "feel" in the usual sense. I feel something, but not precisely what I expect I should. Except incessant pins and needles, tightness, hyper-sensitivity. Most materials feel odd. And if I rub the fingers of one hand against the fingers of the other, the feeling is a hybrid of velvety and raspy. I have been sewing, thinking this would be good for my fine motor control. Of late I have made a small quilt, a jumper, a t-shirt, a skirt, two pairs of pants, and a camisole. I still have no real sewing hands, and I still cannot recognize a pin to the touch with anything but my eyes. Interesting how much easier it is to sew than to knit. Knitting is really tricky. Stitches drop and go unnoticed if one's eyes are not on the work. I think I must keep my hands working. It is a kind of self-conducted oc-cupational therapy, in hopes of maintaining as much capability as I can.

Am I lazy? It must look like I am simply lazy. That is how it appears to me. I start with enthusiasm. I feel good. See how good my balance is, how steady my legs are? Humph! Thirty minutes can change all that. Lumpidty, lumpidty back to the house from the garden. The whoopsie shuffle, here we go again. I am impatient with myself. I am not in the mood for a break. A break is sweet relief after a morning's labors . . . and lunch to satisfy a hearty appetite. That is what a break is for.

There is nothing that is fun to eat. Rich and ordinary indulgences denied because the wretched disease doesn't like saturated fat. I have learned the truth of this because I have felt the after-effects of eating these rich foods. The effects are real and long-lasting. Everything tempting that I love has saturated fat. Chocolate. Butter. Cheesecake. Lunenburg sausage. Pork hocks and turnip kraut. Beef Wellington. Lasagna. Greek spinach pie. Sour cream peach pie. Homemade ice cream. Have an apple? I love apples. There are at least eight kinds I particularly like. Maybe a piece of celery? A carrot? Grapes? Pita? Rice cake? I like these things, too, but the taste buds yearn for a little indulgence. How about a marshmallow? Marshmallows have no fat, but they are only good roasted on the beach, when a little sand adds to the experience. For a treat, I have taken to eating popsicles, twizzalators. I hate twizzalators. I shall definitely quit the twizzalators. Panda licorice has no fat, and I like it a lot. I rarely have any around. Oh yes, go easy on the sugar! This is what the MS cookbook says. No saturated fat, stick to unsaturated fat, and go easy on the sugar. Brother. I love food. I love to cook. How carefully I trim the meat into leanness. I have discovered low-fat frozen yogurt and chocolate gelato. They are better than ice cream. I think I am wonderfully wicked to discover something that is better than the thing I cannot have!

I am turning over a new leaf. All because of my love for cheese, and there's fat for you! I've tried the "low-fat cheeses" (oxymoron), but their taste bears a shocking resemblance to their plastic wrapper! No! I want Brie, Camembert, Stilton, Cheshire, Boursin, Gruyère, feta, Swiss, Oka, Gouda, Cheddar—very old with Kalamata olives—and all the rest, too. I have decided that rather than eat the low-fat, reasonable facsimile of cheese frequently, I shall save up for a delightful piece of real cheese. I don't mind the wait. This, my reward for surviving in between without it. Not only that, I shall celebrate in a modest fashion whenever the occasion calls for celebration, and grant myself temperate tastes of shortbread or chocolate malt and maybe even the odd truffle. I am very good at dreaming up excuses to celebrate.

On the good side, I have learned to drink my coffee black. No cream—17.5% butterfat. Just plain black. Better that way—Ethiopian, Sumatran, Burundian, Guatemalan, Costa Rican (it is a theme of ours—a love of bold coffee) from PEI Coffee Roasters. Smooth. Rich. Wonderful. Two cups in the morning. We love it that some of the best coffee in the world is freshly roasted and ground, just down the road, in rural Prince Edward Island.

Michael sometimes eats liver and eggs and potato salad for breakfast. We all look aghast at that.

Sleep

Daytime sleep has never appealed to me. It seemed there were quite a lot of more interesting things I could do with a day. I have a husband who can fall asleep most anywhere. The most amazing to me were his Saturday afternoon "I'll just have a half-hour catnap" snoozes, except the catnap was on the living-room floor with three preschoolers crawling over him, and it lasted for hours. When they got a little older, the kids figured out if they made themselves scarce they could stretch a Saturday nap into decent play time rather than chore time. To me, Saturday afternoon was not a chance to slip into a sleep, but a choice opportunity to work on "The List." Everybody has "The List," and if some attempt is not made to attack the top of it, the bottom of it will grow longer and longer, deeper and deeper, into the realm of the impossible. Some things on "The List" need a team.

I remember never liking to nap as a child, and as a grown-up the idea was anathema. This napping of Michael's drove me to distraction so that I did not think sensibly. I saw the socks behind the bathroom door as villains and the empty juice jugs in the fridge as delinquents. However . . .

I was about to learn something. I learned about fatigue that hits most inappropriately and inopportunely. MS is the master of fatigue. It has got it down to an art form. It comes like a pall dropping over the head, falling down to the feet, completely shrouding one in its power. A mantle, a heavy mantle out of which there is no escape. There is no shield against the pall of MS fatigue. The only choice is to succumb to it. Ah! Sleep. Suddenly, sleep was something to do, an activity almost. "Go fly a kite!" to everything else!

Well, there it was. Suddenly the possibility of being tired in the middle of a good day seemed not treachery but unimpeachable correctness as a response to the demands of being alive. Now it made sense to me how a Saturday afternoon nap was a reasonable response to the twelve hundred small decisions teachers make in a day, every day, and which are a prime factor in teachers' exhaustion. Mea culpa.

A big part of me still hates the daytime nap because it isn't a willful choice but a succumbing to the inevitable. But I did soften my position about The Nap. About this time Michael turned into (as he says) "a tough old dog" and found unexpected stamina. Something about being needed. It made me remember that while my husband might need a little extra sleep, there is nobody who will stay with a job to the bitter end like he will. There are nap times. There are awake times. Both he embraces with characteristic savoir faire. *Par exemple*:

One day, his mother noticed her engagement ring was not on the windowsill over the kitchen sink. She knew it had been there, and after looking carefully about, suspected the worst. An investigation revealed it was not in the under-sink drainpipe.

Knowing there was not any other possibility, they realized the ring had, indeed, gone down the drain. Michael dug till the septic tank was uncovered, removed the top, and, together, he and his mother began the awful job of emptying the tank, bucketful by bucketful. When it was empty, and the ring had not been found, they searched carefully on the bottom of the tank until finally—there it was! The ring. The treasured engagement ring her sweetheart had given her so many years before had been recovered with the help of her eldest son. Love in action, to the bitter end. No sleepy day. No nap. You can't nap when you are truly needed. I got it.

Except for one thing—I don't like rest. I'd rather be digging.

The Care Package

It wasn't Christmas, or birthday, or anniversary. Just a regular, plain day. Connie delivered the package right to the door. Of course it would be from Helen. Who but Helen would create and send a package when there wasn't anything to celebrate, except that she is my heart-sister? Helen Patricia Mackenzie Steinberg, a good Charlottetown girl. Island born and bred. We are not connected by birth, but we certainly are connected at the heart, ever since we were young, feisty, crazy, and cute. Helen was impossibly cute. Later, we meant to write a book about college and then the hilarious days when our kids were all little. We still could. Helen is very funny. Naturally funny. She simply can't help it. Now this current damnable exacerbation had her needing to do something. She lives too far away—Ontario. This is a big country. And so a care package arrived. Vintage HP. I call her HP sometimes. That'd be Helen Patricia. Not Hewlett Packard.

You have to receive a care package from Helen to really appreciate her creative turn of mind. An e-mail preceded the package. It read: " . . . coming soon to a 'pope's toffice' (Corrie's description at two) near you:

1: something mindless for your tired brain, to read on the facility or wherever, when you want to do something one step above vegetating,

2: something for your tired spirit, when the Magnificent Splendor leaves you feeling alone and you need a quick connection to Heaven,

3: someone to make you smile, and to watch over you when I'm not there, and to make you feel comforted on rainy Mondays when no-longer-little ones are far away in Halifax,

4: something to put on when you just have to run down to the corner, for a bit of whatever, and you'd prefer not to wear that one with the spaghetti sauce,

5: something to sip and savour, on a quiet spring evening, when the sun is sinking and so are you,

6: something that seems to be an indulgence but isn't because it's low-cal and lasts and lasts, unless you chew (not rude, either),

7:    a little bit of light for atmosphere on those quiet spring evenings when the no-longer-little ones are away, and the no-longer-young one isn't, and he's still hot, after all those years."

The box contained: the current issue of *People* magazine, a book of Mother Theresa's, a teddy bear with wings, a t-shirt with a garden on it, some herbal tea, licorice, scented candles.

Helen had signed the note, "So, enjoy, girl. Love ya, Me."

Me too you, Helen, me too you.

"Mother Beloved"

It happened on Sunday morning, the day after Tom, Lissa, Michael, and I celebrated our mother's seventy-fifth birthday with her. We had arrived unannounced, a live surprise with cake and presents in arms. We had made the trip to the North Shore of New Brunswick in order that the occasion be a memorable one, so that not only the surprise but the offering of ourselves as gift would linger in her memory through the long winter days which followed her November birthday.

Unexpectedly, she had a gift for us. An extraordinary gift, and it was planned. She had prepared it. Somehow she knew we would come. And so we accompanied her to church on Sunday morning. She was to sing a solo. We sat in the nave, and a voice floated over us from the balcony. A pure, sweet, rich voice filled with life and force and courage, singing "Mother Beloved."

She sang that at St. Mary's when we lived in Oregon. As a little girl, I loved being up in the balcony with the choir, looking down on the scene below, listening to my mother sing. And here, now, was that voice, the very same one. It seemed she had taken a step back in time through the medium of her voice so that she was thirty-five, not seventy-five, for it was a young voice. In it, the memory of us playing in the yard, a delighted Mum watching, laughing, with applause for our tricks, and there was lemonade.

Tom and I looked at each other, and in that glance shared how moved we were that we could hear all the virtue and beauty in her life sung into this song; touched to hear her reach so deep and with such fire. It was for us. It was "I love you" and everything else. We knew we were the only ones who would understand the significance of "Mother Beloved." A birthday gift, hers for us, an ethereal moment, one I shall always treasure.

Travel/Bamako

Cecily called from New Zealand last evening, which was this morning there. Fiji was amazing. She loved the fact that it is so undeveloped (for tourism) on the tiny outer islands. Outhouses, the very basics. She was plunked into the heart of the place. She said it was perfect. The last two days she was in a resort on Viti Levu Island. She said that was very boring and that she would never stay in a resort again, especially alone. Six more hours, and she would be in Australia.

Travel when you are young, I tell them, as much as you can. Travel when you are young with legs. Legs are critical as that is the biggest part of the adventure, the walking. So one can look up close, hear and smell and see the place and meet the people.

When I was her age I was in French West Africa.

There was a promise I made to myself not to forget Bamako, ever. Of all the places I saw in French West Africa, this city, the capital of Mali, left me with the clearest images of the things I must know. I was on an International Seminar with World University Service of Canada. We left home the middle of June, and when we got to Paris there was some intensive reorientation as we were diverted from Senegal to Morocco because of political strife. It wasn't believed to be safe for a group of Canadian students to be traveling there when Senegalese students were rioting. We did extensive travel in Morocco and were in Mali before continuing on to Ivory Coast. We would be home by the first of September, in time to return to college. I was nineteen years old when we arrived in Mali. I do remember all those images, and often enough to give me strength and focus. Now I know why I need these memories and where the treasure lies in them.

It was hot, that July, and the Niger River was high after the rainy season so that there was a risk from the mosquitoes. They didn't bother me as much as the rhinoceros beetles, which were huge and fierce-looking. For these I stepped aside. The roads in Bamako were dusty. Everything was dusty. It was good to go into the cathedral, out of the sun, for Sunday Mass. The cathedral had a dirt floor to kneel on. The ground was warm and powdery, a soft sandy color. There were long benches for seats, which were a little tippy. Very tippy. Except for this floor and the benches, the cathedral looked, architecturally, much like any other I'd been in: tall, so the sound had a place to go. All of a sudden, in the midst of Mass, singing broke out. There was no choir because the congregation was the choir. I was fascinated to hear what I could distinguish as about six harmonic parts. How was this learned? Obviously, everybody bursts into song out of the heart. Who directs? These were hearts that were in tune. You cannot reproduce the feeling of this joyful song on a recording. You can't capture enough energy, in its fullness, on a recording, and clearly this was energy offered to praise God, and it was glorious! Why can't we sing like this at home? I think because we don't sing all day—working, walking, playing—we don't get to practise singing as a response to living, with the harmony of our shared trials.

We were lodged at the Normal School, where teachers are trained. It sat on a hill overlooking the Niger River. One supper I took a place in the dining room at a table with three African students. Something awful was placed on the table for supper. I asked what the dish was called and was told, *"Poulet avec la sauce arachnide,"* and I gulped. Chicken with spider sauce. It was feasible.

"Pardon?"

"Poulet avec la sauce arachnide."

I dropped my napkin and picked it up, feigning a miss of that response, and asked a third time.

"Poulet avec la sauce arachide," came a clearer reply. It is difficult to understand French when spoken with a Bambara accent.

"Ah oui, c'est bien!" Chicken with peanut sauce. It didn't matter any more what it looked like.

We were given time in the Bamako library to do research. Such an interesting building—not large, but unusual when compared to local architecture. I remember it being off by itself, with trees all around, and we needed the bus to get to it. Curious, a library so far away from the people. Many of the books were very large and very old, so that they had to be handled gingerly.

On July 13 we attended a special performance of the Bamako Ballet, which ended with many of us on the stage for the final dance. It was my twentieth birthday, which is how I can remember the date. Quite a birthday.

Finally, the day came to visit the leper colony. It was easy to know something about the lepers because they were most places, living their lives with this terrible affliction. One night there had been a traditional concert with musicians and dancers, many of whom were missing toes, a part of a nose or fingers, lost at the joint as happens with leprosy. I bought a string of beads from an old man in the street who was a leper. He had a big basket of beautiful beads which he had strung in wonderful arrangements on thin, strong cord. I chose a necklace and thanked him. He smiled a big, toothless smile. I didn't know there was a bead on that necklace that glowed in the dark. That was a surprise. I always wished I could have thanked him, specially, for that bead. I wore the necklace for years, and one day the cord broke. I put all the beads in a small, green box. After some time I decided to re-string them, even though I felt this was one disconnection from the old man who made the necklace. I have not had to re-string them again. That one bead still glows in the dark.

I was thinking about him when we arrived at the leper colony. It was located on the outskirts of Bamako where there were wide-open spaces and baobab trees. In the compound there was a village made of small, concrete block houses and a hospital nearby, several buildings in a cluster. Along the outside wall of one of the buildings, there was a blackboard. In front of this the children sat cross-legged on the ground for their school lessons. The teacher was a Gray Nun. The children were of all ages.

The village was built for families with leprosy. The healthiest parent stayed in the house with the children, while the other parent was in hospital for treatment. This way, everyone got treatment—the less ill maintaining some semblance of family life; the seriously ill receiving treatment while still being able to see the family. The nurses, Gray Nuns from Quebec, looked after everyone. The physicians were from Quebec as well.

First, we went on a tour of the hospital. There were long wards with beds facing each other along both walls. The walls were painted a soft green; I remembered that. There were large windows, too, on both sides, so that the rooms were bright and as close to the outside activity as possible. We met all the patients, who greeted us with warm smiles and glad hellos. They showed us their ailing limbs or festering skin, as the nurses explained specifics of the disease—how long patients had been there and what the prognosis was. I realized they were showing us how proud they were of their improvement, not the least ashamed of their deformity. Then we were given a class on the nature, progression, and treatment of the disease, with slides that showed us the remarkable success that had been achieved with patients in this treatment center. A young man of about twenty years old came in to show us the extraordinary change in his skin since treatment had begun. We had seen on the slides what he looked like several years earlier.

The treatment offered here had been pioneered by this medical team from Canada. They had worked here for many years and were not the least concerned about succumbing to the disease themselves. Infection occurs after persistent, long-term physical contact, which explains why entire families become afflicted. Early intervention provides the best chance to halt the disease, and so an education program formed an important part of the work of this little order of nuns. If they could get people for treatment early on, they could cure them. What happened to themselves was immaterial. I could see they felt safe enough, because of precautions taken, and the threat of the disease posed no impediment to their enthusiasm. It was an incredible example of self-emptying love. This, secure in the heart and evidenced in the eyes, is a wonderful sight. This, I must not, will not, ever forget.

It was sunset when we prepared to leave the leper colony. The sky was orange, pink, gold. The sun was dropping down behind the baobab, so that it was silhouetted like a beautiful, great, black sculpture against a wall of fire. It stood as a guard over a community where the impossible was possible, where gladness reigned, where love conquered everything. I took a picture of that tree.

Sometimes people ask how I am coping with my own disease, and I remember the baobab.

The Knot Garden

Body bound in a manicured knot garden,
clipped boxwood hedging around
lavender, rue, hyssop—
unable to escape, till chance yielded a break
allowed a determined departing, unnoticed.

Years later the field beside blew
with lavender,
And no one knew it was
a spirit running free.

6 ❧ EPISODES AND EVENTS

The Music Books

The phone rang. It was 3:30 p.m. "Mom, it's me. I'm at Mrs. McBurnie's for my piano lesson, but I forgot to take my music books to school with me. I got off the bus here anyway. What should I do?"

Hmmm. Life is hard when you are six. Della had arrived to baby-sit the other two, as I planned on going for a run. "I could run the books up to you. Can you give me fifteen or twenty minutes? Would that be okay, Geth?"

"Okay. Then I can take my lesson second, after Erin."

I changed for my run, stretched, put the backpack with the music books on and headed down the lane and turned onto the road. No matter how you begin from this point there is an uphill beginning to the run. I checked my watch. It was such a beautiful day. I flew down the road, past the Pinette Women's Institute building and the marsh, up the hill past Larsen's farm, on to McBurnies', and down their long lane. I knocked on the door and handed the books to one pleased little boy.

"Thanks, Mom!" Was that admiration I saw?

"No trouble, Gethin, really. It is a fine day for a run."

I ran home. I checked my watch at the bottom of our lane. It is a four-and-a-half-mile run, round rip. I had done it in thirty-two minutes. Seven-minute miles. Not bad.

MS can take my legs, but it can't take that run from me.

Back on the Ward

I'd been daydreaming to pass the time in the hospital. Being there for only Solu-Medrol, time passes slowly. Unlike past experiences, this round of steroids proved to be very painful in the receiving. It was bloody uncomfortable enduring the IV; the solution hurt, coursing though my veins like fire. I wanted to pull it out. I had not experienced this in the past. But there I was, in the hospital. I'd have to carry through to the finish.

I finally fell asleep in that noisy, uncomfortable place. The atmosphere was sterile, the air stultifying. Home was sweet, delicious, cozy. As I drifted off, I tried to forget anything more. Don't think! I thought. I didn't like the way the story only got worse.

I went home after five doses of Solu-Medrol, not feeling one whit better than when I went in, and possibly worse, except that the headaches were gone. I arrived at the hospital in a wheelchair. I left in a wheelchair. I was not impressed. I was affronted even. The next day I was feeling worse than ever. I had bright red cheeks, which might be mistaken for a rosy glow. Rosy glow, all right. I was on fire. I was glad I was not given to panic. And the next day, Sunday, my bright red cheeks were flaming red. Now not a glow, but a blaze. What was happening? I was terribly weak, barely able to lift my head from the pillow, and I had an overwhelming feeling of uneasiness. Some Christmas magician!

On Monday Dr. Flanagan called the MS Clinic in Halifax and was advised that there are instances of adverse reaction to Solu-Medrol. It would pass. I could go to the hospital for two more days of treatment (forget that!!) in the hopes it might help. But better to wait it out. That I did, and in several days I was feeling only as bad as I had upon entering the hospital. This was progress. I could get from bed to bathroom, and the rest (meals, laundry, housework) Michael and Eric saw to cheerfully. I know they were trying to encourage me.

Since I could not get downstairs, I spent the time pleasantly, profitably, in my Bower. Winter now, the Treehouse became a bower, the Treehouse being too chilly. Eric delivered a lunch tray before he left for school each day. I entertained friends, who knew to come right upstairs. "Would you like some tea? Yes? Well, you may go make it!" One day my very dear friends, Lynn MacDonald and Annie Carter, came to see me. I missed them. We had shared years of watching our children, all the same age, grow up, while we mothers supported each other. We sit in a row in the soprano pew in choir. I am in the middle with Lynn on the left and Annie on the right. Since I have had MS I have, over the years, managed to miss a bit of everything—practices, Advent Carol Service, Christmas Midnight Mass, Easter Vigil, Ascension, Patronal Festival, choral Evensong, and choir parties. Not one person in the St. Peter's Cathedral Choir has ever complained about absenteeism, but rather each has sent hugs home to me via Michael. Now I was very happy to see these two faces arrive with treats and a bottle of Harvey's Bristol Cream! This was shaping up to be a good day after all. So I had one cautious, small glass of sherry, and I was instantly a goner. My cheeks fired up. We laughed and laughed. We thought this was very funny. Everything sounded funny. I thought it was hilarious. Sherry with morning coffee?

With no vision problems (after Eric devised a reading stand to use in bed since I couldn't get a good hold on a book), I had free reign to read all day if I chose. My good friend Wayne, Dr. Hankey, sent me *Teresa of Avila,* and I quietly absorbed *The Interior Castle* in the way a contemplative book takes thoughtful time, and then *The Way of Perfection.* Dr. Hankey is generous to me with teaching. He is a professor of Classics at Dalhousie University. An internationally known philosopher and theologian, he is the acknowledged world authority on Thomas Aquinas. Once, on a winter visit with us, he devoted the weekend to a seminar on Boethius' *Contemplation of Philosophy* just for me. We sat around the fire, and he taught between walks in the snowy woods. (My numb hands froze.) With *Teresa of Avila* came some lessons in contemplative reading for which I was most grateful. I am quite sure I would never have had the time to give to this study had I not been relegated to the bed. I could see I had a long way to go. Perfection has nothing to do with the world; a lifetime might just about point me in the general direction.

I love my friends. All of them, everywhere.

As for Christmas preparations, well, I had the shopping completed before I got really entrenched in the exacerbation. It is my habit to do this before Advent. And the rest—baking, decorating, cards, and such—these were impossible for me. I learned, peacefully, that the critical preparation for Christmas, the preparation of my heart, can be done from any posture. It was satisfying enough to make my way downstairs, so when the scholars, our children, arrived home, we could visit around the fire.

Exams finished, Gethin and Cecily arrived home from King's. Together with their brother they decorated a big tree and all the house. They cleaned and baked and were the busiest Christmas angels one could know. They did it all, as their Dad was bidden away to another family reunion. It wasn't usual for Michael to be away so close to Christmas, but his younger brother was being sworn in as a judge in Ontario, so this was an extra-special event. When he returned, Michael walked into a Christmas Eve home. Thus was I humbled into mellow composure.

While Midnight Mass was out of the question for me, I did make it to Christmas Morning Mass. And this without a cane. Together we made our traditional Christmas dinner, not one omission. I had decided I'd be happy with any adjustments to the menu, considering the circumstances. But no. They insisted I play the role of chef, directing my sous-chefs, who worked like a well-oiled machine. I had the routine in my head. I made the cucumber mousse that was the first cooking I had done since mid-November.

By the end of the Christmas holiday, the numbness was receding and the tight band disappearing. During the course of the exacerbation, since I was numb anyway, I had decided to forgo the child's dosage of Zoloft I was taking as a muscle relaxant for my back pain. It had been very effective. It was a thin possibility Barb thought I should try. It worked. The back pain and spasms disappeared. The drug especially relieved the feeling that somebody was pushing me from behind—a feeling that may be okay if you can run to keep up with yourself but that, since I can't accelerate, knocked me off balance. Very precarious. Yet, I abandoned Zoloft altogether when January arrived, and I was decidedly out of the grips of the thing. This did leave me with some back tightness, but I was determined to start swimming in February and wanted to know what the real effect of this exercise might be. Also, I was getting impatient with the decrease in sexual responsiveness caused by the Zoloft and knew (through my extensive research) that it takes five days without Zoloft to regain that responsiveness.

More than once a pharmacist asked me, "Why are you taking a child's dose or half a child's dose?" "Because it is for muscle pain in my back, not for depression," I explained. One pharmacist was so interested in this approach, we had a great visit, during which he gave me a little bottle with two child's dose pills in it—"left here, not much demand, so you can have them"—and then he forgot to give me my prescription. But he called me at home when he discovered the mistake and offered to deliver them—to Belfast! I said, "Don't be silly, I'll get them next time I am in town!" People are so willing.

I always wondered if Zoloft would work in reverse, which concerned me. Would it make a contented me a depressed me? My doctor assured me it did not do this, and she was right.

Still, I hated the drug.

Pedal

A bright idea might hit at any moment and one did. I inveigled Eric's assistance, and, duly, there was air once again in the formerly flat tires of the bicycle. I was in search of moss to line the hanging baskets so I could get them planted, and I was determined to get the moss myself. It was pretty shaky going at first, for it had been years since I was on a bike. Poor balance. But away I went. It got better. I set out in the direction of the hollow. This was downhill, after which I'd continue into the woods and gather the needed moss. All at once I was overcome with sudden liberty, moving freely and swiftly. How can one explain the sheer delight and thrill of speed after years of being locked in a body for which acceleration has been an impossibility? This was it, the answer. I would travel on a bicycle. Everything would be different now. Fast and free.

As I rounded the corner at the bottom of the hill, my shoe flew off and I lost my balance and crashed. It was a respectable, "professional wipe-out"—as the kids were wont to call a decent, not wimpish, tumble. I got back on the bike knowing things were not exactly as I had imagined for those few glorious seconds. I could not make the bike go. Truth is, you need two working legs to ride a bike, not one. You can't pedal uphill with one leg. I thought I would disintegrate, but I still needed the moss. I knew there was some nearby and I went to gather it, leaving the bicycle behind. Then I rejoined the bike and pushed it back up the hill from the hollow to the bottom of the lane. Now I sat down and wept. My new dream was over as fast as it had begun. My wonderful dream of independence with the wind in my face because of my own speed—vanquished. I pushed the bike the rest of the way home. I felt so sad all day. I remembered the wonderful feeling, over and over, with my astonished joy at its appearance, and how badly I wanted to repeat it. Michael says I could pedal down the lane, abandon the bike, and he would bring it back so I could go down again. But that defeats my whole purpose. It was the independence that beguiled me. And I'd only have to walk back up the lane.

Well, I got the moss. The hanging baskets looked fine. I planted coleus, bocapa, and ivy in them.

Illusion

Illusion, according to the Oxford dictionary, is "deception, delusion; sensuous perception of an external object involving a false belief; a transparent tulle (fine silk net used for veils and dresses)." I know all about illusion. It is living in me.

It was July and hot. I lay on the bed. I was not able to go any place else, being in the midst of an event. I was waiting to see when I would be able to pit reality against illusion by watching the sheet rise at the bottom of the bed over my feet. My legs and feet felt as if they were swollen to an incredible size so that they created an incline upwards from my knees to my feet. Yet the covers lay flat on my outstretched legs. I couldn't see anything odd. So I whipped the sheet back and there they were, as normal as could be, just resting there on the bed. Illusion.

Then it was September, and along came another event. This time I owned a suit of armor, a full suit from my shoulders to my toes. It was the wrong size, much too small, and the boots were particularly ill-fitted. My toes were wrapped under my feet so that it hurt like blazes to stand up because my toes were crushed under my full weight. Nevertheless, crawling was not an option because the armor made that too painful. This was the first time I admitted that MS really could be painful. When I looked in the mirror there was no suit of armor, and when I looked down my toes were just where they should be. Yet it was a mission getting back to bed. My poor feet. Just an illusion.

Early on in my MS experience, some cardboard attached itself to the soles of my feet with crazy-glue. It is about the thickness of the cardboard that forms the backing on a pad of writing paper. It crinkles when I wiggle my toes. At first it was a terrible annoyance, and I wanted to tear it off. But since it wasn't really there I could hardly do that. After eight months or so I was mostly forgetting about it. And now, years later, I suppose I would feel awfully weird if the beastly cardboard disappeared. I'd probably miss it. I like to go barefooted all summer, around the farm. The grass feels good, better than usual, better than shoes. So the good thing is, in spite of the fact my feet are quite numb to my ankles, I still feel the sensation of grass—cool, soft grass—beneath my feet. I like this.

Just the other afternoon Michael called out, "See the rainbow." It wasn't raining and the sky was blue, dove blue with myriad pink clouds floating in it. The sun was beginning its descent in the western sky. East, from the place where the river narrows into the woods, there was a rainbow. It was wide and clear so that red, orange, yellow, green, blue, indigo, violet arched in flawless succession. It was so big we had to walk around the yard till we found the other end straight across the river from the south side of the house. And then, standing at the edge of the three-cornered field, we could see it all, start to finish, the most stately perfect rainbow we had ever seen. We felt as though we had stepped into the pages of a child's picture book. Till it disappeared. Illusion.

I liked the part about illusion as transparent tulle. Maybe a rainbow is tulle in the sky.

Trip Through Spring

As planned, one February to May, I swam. My back improved greatly. The experiment worked. But then May arrived, and my legs were too weary and too weird to do the deep-water workout, and the water temperature in the pool had been raised till it was uncomfortably warm and turned me into a noodle. They made it warm like that for the arthritis class. The competitive swim team and synchronized swim team preferred cold water.

I tried weight lifting, but after four sessions knew that it was not worth the effort of the drive to the fitness center. After each session I felt depleted, not energized. Dragged myself home. Maybe I was doing something wrong, who knows? It was always the same, no matter what I tried. Everything made me feel worse. In any case, not wanting to give up, I decided I could do as well at home, and save time and travel. That was worth something to me, since everything added to the fatigue. I tried resistance work with surgical tubing. Very boring, though I understood the boring part came from having to do it alone. Fitness needs a friend. A surgical tube was not much of a friend.

Next, there was yoga. Maintaining discipline is a problem when you have MS because everything is hard and makes you feel worse, so there is no incentive to stick with it when you get no physical payback. I guess a trainer would give one a good swift boot. A trainer would be good. I only ever really loved running and skiing because those are outdoors. Or dancing, because that was beautiful. So next, I held a dance class with myself as the sole pupil. You can do barre work without great balance. Perfect. I put on the music, and I had so much fun I overdid it and had trouble going down stairs for a week. I figured I'd probably try again, but with a lid on the enthusiasm.

That spring was a nasty one. Cold, so cold, and wet. The spring and I have our troubles together. It is so often like this. Spring is bad, I am bad. Spring is good, I am bad. Rarely does it happen that spring is good and I am good. I have not found anybody who can enlighten me beyond "the change of seasons is particularly difficult for someone with MS." I already knew that much. I know I can depend on something happening in spring, and I always hope the next spring will be better. I'm forever putting my hope in the next spring. How can I get from winter to summer, unscathed? I start to think about it as March ends. I have a lot of gardening to do in spring, and feeling bad is a terrible intrusion. It wrecks my plan.

Well, after a good month's rest I resumed swimming. I was glad to be there again. I enjoyed so much the camaraderie of my neighbors Hazel Davies, Linda MacLeod, and Margaret MacRae. Our little foursome ranged in age from thirty to seventy-five. It was the seniors who were the inspiration. What fun we all had with the class. There were twenty-four of us, if we were all there. Gus said one morning as I got into the pool, "Everybody wants to know why we all got fat and you stayed thin!" If he only knew how I really feel. How would he like to be thin with no muscle tone? It is pathetic to me. Nevertheless, a half-decent effort would be made with "brawny" as a healthy goal. I used to be strong. I suspected brawny was impossible, while puny was very doable! After the first truly nasty exacerbation, when swallowing and using cutlery was difficult, I weighed 115 pounds and scared even myself.

That spring when I was writing a report for Jock, some notes for my file, I fibbed. Not an out-and-out lie, just stretching it, but it was amusing all the same. I had my annual physical right after lunch—and a delicious, big lunch too! One is weighed fully clothed, shoes and all, so those factors gave me a weight of 128 pounds (my muscled weight when I was a runner). It sounded so much more robust than the actual 122 pounds, that I claimed it as the truth, wishing of course the extra weight was muscle, and I included it in my update along with the ordinary true stats—hemoglobin and stuff.

In life, there are surprises. Wonderful, touching surprises. That season became the spring of our own miracle of the loaves and fishes. In the worst of it, my friend, Glenda Cooper, arrived with a baked ham and scalloped potatoes. Not only was it the most delicious of such ever tasted, so that it has become the standard by which the family judges all ham and scalloped potatoes, but it was of such surprising proportions it lasted for days and days and days, which meant nobody, and I mean nobody, had to worry about supper all that time.

I wanted to feel hearty. I wanted a spring in glorious contrast to the miserable one last year, and I wanted to be in it. But drat, another May arrived and with it a revival, an unwelcome revival, of those typical symptoms so common in spring. Once again, getting from winter through spring to summer proved difficult. Again, always again, and again. A tight band of about six inches in width gripped my waist with varying intensity, depending upon my level of fatigue. My right leg reprised its role as "hemlock leg." How thou dost fail me! My hands continued to be numb. One day, I found a small sticker on the end of my index finger, and I had no idea how long it had been there, or how it got there. In fact, I never did get feeling back, even after last spring's IV vitamin therapy, which claimed some efficacy for numb hands. I suppose I might have kept that up longer, but it was such a job. It required several hours at the doctor's office during which a battle royal was waged to find a decent vein for the IV. Not much fun. (One would wonder by what matter of conveyance blood was carried through my body.) The time, the drive, the cost—it was all just too much. If I had big, plump veins I think we could have done it at home, but, as it was, a nurse and doctor had difficulty, so I wouldn't think of putting Michael through a task that was a trial for the experts. He would think he was torturing me, what with all the bruising. Once in a while, but never when I need them, there were excellent veins. How this tired me.

All these spring symptoms felt like a replay of an exacerbation I knew very well, not so intense that I was completely stopped in my tracks, but lingering in slow retreat. An echo. An unwelcome echo. Is this what was meant by "progressive"? I wondered. If this were a board game, it would come without any rules. MS is so often invisible, yet so universally feared for the moment it might become visible in someone else, or present in oneself. I must see it as something else. It was about this time that I found the Magnificent Splendor. There are a lot of us in it.

B&B—No Heritage Inn

The B&B experience is a charming one. It can be had in a country estate, a seaside retreat, a village cottage. But there is another B&B, and eventually it happens to everyone who has MS. It might be a major difficulty or a minor annoyance, but definitely B&B: bladder and bowel. It's the thing one does not want to mention, not in polite company in any case. They referred to it in all the books, so I was anticipating possible loss of bladder control or even complete incontinence. Not me. Instead I clung to my water. I could read three chapters of *War and Peace* while waiting for bladder let-down. Thus, I discovered I am not a patient person. I thought I was patient, but this tried me to the limit. It was not my intent to wile away perfectly good time in the loo. The joke was on me because I had nothing to say about it.

It was a bit like rediscovering the coping mechanisms one had in abundance when there were babies in the house. Babies love to wet themselves, or, better yet, soil their diapers just as they are being bundled up for an outing. Off with boots, snow suit, hat, mitts, and change the diaper. Baby looks at you with sweet eyes (relief) and rosy, soft cheeks (extreme youth), dimpled hands swinging around in the air. Now, as I was ready to step out the door I realized there must (must, must, must, you never know) be one last visit to the loo. This was a newly learned, just-in-case reflex: just in case I need to go halfway to town, just in case I need to go while doing errands, just in case I need to go in the middle of church, just in case I really do need to go. It usually did feel like I could go. Damn. Maybe next time.

Then there came the week this changed character for the worse, for I had the urge, all the time, right around the clock. Twenty-four hours in a row of damn, damn, damn. A pitiful stream, a painful burn with its arrival, and no relief as I suffered through the week. Of course it would be Holy Week, and the choir sings nine services between Palm Sunday Mass and Easter Sunday Evensong. There was a lot of sweating going on during Tenebrae. I doubted I would make it through Easter Vigil.

So on Holy Saturday I went to the pharmacy. I walked through the aisle with the discreet adult products. Depends and Poise—who names this stuff? Just happened to be in the aisle on my way to the vitamins, of course. I glanced at the labels surreptitiously, not wanting to appear the least bit interested or needful. "Adult protection," "safe, dry security brief" (sounds like a good addition to one's portfolio), big pads, little pads, magically hidden pads, pads alone, pads to put on a band or even full panties. Ingenious. There was a wall of this stuff. I couldn't bear it. And I wasn't going to fork over good money for a box of it. Maybe one pad, in an unmarked package. I only needed one to get me through Easter Vigil. No, this was ridiculous. I didn't need this stuff. I won't need this stuff. Couldn't bear it. I couldn't even bear pausing in the aisle. How often did this wall get stocked? Security risk? No, no, no! No security briefs for me. What was it about these things? Why? Why so timid to face the possibility that one needs such help? Was it a loss of dignity, decorum, propriety? Or the loss of control over one's body? Scary. I left with relief.

I thought I should still have a measure of protection of a modest sort. I put on two ultra thin maxipads. Feminine hygiene products, quite acceptable. That should do it. The Easter Vigil was moving and beautiful, as always. It wasn't till it was over that I realized I had not given a thought to my condition. It was gone. What relief when I realized it was over. I recovered. Comfort indescribable. It is true—it is the little things in life that make all the difference.

I recovered completely. However, a couple months later, at my annual physical, I found out that it bore the clear stamp of a bladder infection, and once again I learned not all of life's annoyances are attributable to MS. But I had recovered on my own. No antibiotic. And I thought that was pretty neat.

It wasn't the first time I had wrongly attributed peculiar things to MS. There was the shoulder event. A brisk, rasping sound accompanied by a fiery streak through my upper arm accosted me as I flung a bag of stuff into the rear seat of the car. There were some amazing illusions accompanying this disease, but this one was very dramatic. I saw it as one of the cruder hoaxes I had yet experienced. Of course, once was not enough, so there were repeat performances off and on for several weeks. Then my shoulder quit working. I had a limited arch just in front of me through which my arm could move, but that was it.

I waited patiently to recover, but to no avail. So after two months I took my shoulder to my doctor. Barb said, "You know you can still hurt yourself. This is not illusion. I am always amazed with the things my patients with chronic illness are prepared to endure because they think it is nothing more than another annoying symptom. Well, you have a frozen shoulder as a result of a torn muscle in your arm between your shoulder and elbow. The frozen shoulder is a response to the injury. With only a little movement, the arm has a chance to rest and heal itself." Physiotherapy was sought, but an exuberant therapist ended up making things worse. Next acupuncture. It took away the pain. It didn't take away the pain. It took away the pain. Energy expended to receive the treatments exceeded the length of time the pain was relieved, and I stopped that. Tired. Too tired.

Three more months passed and then I saw the orthopedic surgeon. He pronounced it a classic frozen shoulder and said I should "take heart, as it would be right as rain in about eighteen months, since that is typically how long it takes before a frozen shoulder spontaneously gets better."

I wasn't really counting, but after six months I had just about run out of new and interesting ways to get my arm in a sleeve without killing myself. It was then I took matters into my own hands. To heck with this eighteen-month sentence. Since I knew it couldn't hurt me, and might help, I went on a regime of proanthrocyanadin from grape seed extract. After four days, I had about seventy-five percent of the movement back in my shoulder, so I carried on, and in a short time I had most of my arm and shoulder back. This was spontaneous enough for me and saved me waiting those next twelve months. Who would believe it?

Even so, there are still times when it is tricky to sort out the real from the imaginary. And as for the "&B" part of B&B, I eat All-Bran.

Painting the Bower

It is possible my house-painting career has come to an end. Too bad, because I like painting. In the beginning we wanted to leave the bedroom windows in their natural state—pine. We decided on Swedish Oil to finish them as this would allow painting—if it ever came to that. We like pine since it is indigenous and homey. The winter battle with condensation on the windows—which froze then melted, leaving unsightly mould, no matter what steps for prevention we took—inspired us to paint.

Painting is best a summer job. It is the only opportunity to seize a block of time to work on the bigger house, garden, and woods chores. I had the desire and imagined I had the spunk to do this work. Michael typically had a very long list of things to accomplish during his teacher's summer "off" (haha), so I was impressed when he proposed indoor painting. In summer, windows are dry—perfect for painting—and with windows open, one can breathe with no bother from paint fumes.

The thinking changed from "let's do the windows this year and the rest of the room next year" to "we'll be in the mess anyway, so why not get it all over with?" That was how we got embroiled in a task that mushroomed from the most modest of intentions. We decided that since I sometimes see my entire physical world shrink to the limits of this room, my Bower (winter) or Treehouse (summer), it should be cheerful. Well, it's cheerful all right. I feel now I am in the South Pacific, inviting Paul Gauguin for mango tea. My usual traditional nature was pitched for whimsy, and when finished we had ourselves a Treehouse of very soft, mellow ochre with butter-cream woodwork and coral furniture, to which I added a stuffed coral hassock. It was the coral that saved the whole thing, and that nothing more than a bold hunch. It was much better than the soft dove gray that had been there.

Michael lasted hours on end, all day, but I generally faded after a couple hours of painting. I was able to last that long by doing the sit-down jobs, the furniture (in the barn), and the close-to-the-floor jobs like baseboards. Mind you, my stubborn streak reared up when I finished painting all the wicker and decided I hated it yellow. Too much yellow. That's when I discovered the happy accident of coral, which changed everything. So I started all over again. Wicker is a beggar to paint. A nasty job. The wicker was an antique hand-me-down from my Mum, and I felt a responsibility to make use of it. Never again—wicker. Too much work. Eventually it ended up where it belonged, as porch furniture.

It took a solid, hard week to complete the job. Near the end I declared that as far as I could see, the next painting would only be accomplished by calling in reserves, as it was too much for me. That was a darn shame because I've always liked a good project. Of course there isn't any painter who does such a meticulous, perfect, and clean job as Michael, so maybe . . .

Now, should I get downhearted when in this sunny space I can open my eyes. It is like being in the middle of the late afternoon sun. Also there are at least a hundred books in the room, so there is lots to read, because I haven't finished them all. When I am assigned to this place, I shall be lighthearted. I know I shall have that assignment again, but when? When?

Michael says it makes him feel he is in the tropics, even in the depths of winter. It changes color all day long, and I like that part. Just a little paint, that's all.

Plenty

I remember the day we told the children that their mother has the Magnificent Splendor. They sat, took it in like grave young soldiers, listened carefully to understand. Then, brave and unafraid, announced, "Don't worry. You've always been here for us. Now we will be here for you." That has made all the difference.

It was a rainy day, so I cleaned out a filing cabinet. I found a letter I had written for my family on Thanksgiving 1993. It said:

Dear Michael, Gethin, Cecily, Eric,
My thanksgiving is to you—for all you have given me this year.
You have understood my fears.
You have wrapped me in love.
You have laughed with me, cried with me.
You have brought me bouquets
        planted the garden
        cooked the meals
        cleaned the house
You were my legs, my hands, my eyes.
You prayed with me
        encouraged me
        read to me
        cured me
        uplifted me
And so,
When my outside was
        stumbling, mumbling, blurred
My inside was
        steady, eloquent, clear
For you filled my heart.
        My cup runneth over.

Where love is, God is. Thank you.
> I love you,
> Catherine & Mom   XOXOX

Also in the file there were some "Thanksgiving notes . . . " (Fear of
starvation, I guess.) "Coming home: Gethin and Meg, Vereena (Meg's
friend from Germany), Cecily, Naomi. Eric will be in Sackville. Post
the menu on the fridge. Note what to bake and what to freeze, what
to buy, and which sous-chefs to assign which dishes."

Thanksgiving Weekend Menu 1996

Friday Supper: garden vegetable soup
                      fresh bread
                      apple pie with cheddar or ice cream
                      cider, tea, and coffee

Saturday Breakfast: sticky buns
                      granola
                      yogurt (lemon and cappuccino)
                      juice, coffee

Saturday Lunch: sandwiches: cold cuts/pâté/veggies/cheese
                      cider
                      cookies and squash spice cake
                      apples, pears

Saturday Supper: Greek leg of lamb in garlic, rosemary,
                      and red wine
                      Portuguese mashed potatoes
                      mushroom/onion/fennel casserole
                      beets in dill
                      orange cranberry cake, almond butter cake
                      cider, tea, and coffee

Sunday Breakfast:	juice, coffee, carrot bread
After-church Snack:	olive salsa with pita crackers, cheeses, fruit
Thanksgiving Dinner:	free-range roast turkey (Tony's) apple, raisin, and savory stuffing sherry gravy sweet potato–peach casserole French-cut green beans amandine baked Green Mountains fluffy turnip cucumber mousse fruited coleslaw red wine, apple cider pumpkin cheesecake, whipped cream, and honey coffee/tea

This list was posted on the fridge during Thanksgiving weekend. Everything got cooked and eaten.

Cadence

Early winter landscape in stubble,
brindle grass with snow
             in wind,
a marriage of the remnants of November
with the prospect of December,
in time for bearing the truth.

On the radio, three Ave Marias, one after another.
Bruckner with too many inspirations for one,
divine in music, thought, and inspiration.
             The wind:
landscape and song combine
to devote a time for petit deuil,

a little mourning for something lost,
always a little something more,
graciously, not all at once.
             Like wind,
Providence's rhythm for learning
if suffering is a song or a prayer.

Choristers called early for singing
prepare His arrival.
On the darkest day of winter,
             holy wind.
  "Balulalow, balulalow, balulalow . . .
  and I sall rock Thee in my heart . . . "

Cadence on this holy wind:
a song and a prayer.

7 ❧ THE FLASH

It came unannounced, without fanfare, a complete and perfect feeling of wellness. It took about ten seconds for me to realize what it was. Then a feeling of exhilaration took over me, and I couldn't decide what to do. Walk fast? Jump? Run? Shout for joy? It was after choir practice, walking out to the car. I could walk, like a regular person. Everything worked. Perfectly. I felt well. Utterly well. Then, in a minute, it vanished. Gone. A lightning flash to remind me, to let me remember, what good health was. I knew there was nothing I could do to recreate the feeling. A poignant moment to carry with me, wishing for it to come again. I suppose if I felt like that all the time, knowing what I know now, I would be in a constant state of glee. But I did remember the feeling it harkened back to, now long gone, and it amazed me to think that was how it used to be, that's what it was like. No wonder I could do what I did.

The flash came one more time, just the same and as clearly. I have been waiting for it to visit again, but no. Jill Thompson (a friend who has MS, too) mentioned the other day that it happened to her one summer afternoon on the beach, a thirty-second taste of perfection. How can such a feeling happen? Where does it come from? How can everything be horrible one minute then perfect the next? How odd. How perfectly odd. If it comes again, I hope I am home so that I can have a forty-second run and a twenty-second leap.

People glibly say health is everything. It isn't everything, but it is something. I can't believe it is everything because that would mean I am in deep trouble.

Ballroom Dancing

It was Belinda and Jeff's wedding celebration. There was an excellent dance band and a parquet dance floor. My big brother said to me, "Come on, Cath, let's dance." "Okay." I suspected I could do this—dance, that is. There was someone to hold on to me.

In a flash I remembered the astonishing discovery I made one summer day. Gethin threw his arm around my waist and took off, with me in tow. Worked fine. "Let's try that again." We did. I could run right alongside him. Why, if I cannot accelerate or levitate (the two movements necessary for running), could I, in some basic way, run along holding onto somebody else? I asked Jock. He said it is not a muscle problem, this loss of acceleration, but a loss of "sense in space." If you don't have an idea of where you are in space, it is impossible to move fast. If somebody else can provide this missing sense, then the movement can be accomplished. Well, well. Amazing. But the person has to be the right height. I discovered this. It will not work with a shorter person. The aide must be as tall as or taller than I am.

Tom looked pretty dapper in his tuxedo, father of the bride and all. So away we went. Tom was always a great dancer. I remember he was the heartthrob of dancers in high school because he could dance any dance. Knew them all. He still can dance so, but those days are definitely gone for me. Luckily, Tom invented the "Caribbean Two-Step" for Lissa. This was a short, small-stepped foxtrot he came up with to help Lissa dance after the accident. The doctors said that she would never wake from the coma. She did. They said she would never talk, or walk, or anything. The doctors expected her to stay in bed forever. They said, "She has had 400 to 500 lacerations in her brain. If it was a young brain, it would be a different prognosis. She is 42 and so there is no great hope." Well, they didn't know Lissa! Ever since then, I have wanted to take her back to the hospital to set the record straight, but she has been too busy keeping house, holding down a part-time job, and partying.

Anyway, the Carribean Two-Step was lots of fun. It proved what I suspected all along. It refreshed an idea I brought up on occasion. It went like this: "Michael, I think we should take ballroom dancing. It would be great fun. It think it has possibilities as an activity I could do, because I'd have you to hang on to. Might even work up a sweat. Now there's a thought for you! A little cardiovascular fitness. I know I could never last a whole class without stopping, but we could take rests."

I thought it was a great idea because Michael is a good dancer, and it would be something we could do together. An evening in each other's arms—irresistible. Wrong. Dance classes are on weeknights. Dance classes are in Charlottetown. We are country bumpkins, and one of us is a teacher. Teachers have no energy for dancing at the end of the day. They've been dancing all day in front of a class. And there is marking and preparation because tomorrow is another day of teacher-dance. Rats. But I already knew that. It was only a wild thought. Yet interesting, all the same. I was not given a flat rejection, but "Perhaps when I retire." I shall bring it up again later, if I am still strong enough. The first fall of No School there will be Dance Class. I hope so. He did say an old dream simply needs a new plan. Or, if this is a poor hope, and I cannot dance, there is always the music.

Chopin, Daddy

For my fiftieth birthday I was given the most wonderful CD. Chopin. It is what I wanted. Grande valse, fantasie-impromptu, nocturne, waltz, mazurka, scherzo, étude, polonaise, prelude, ballade, bacarolle. A hundred and thirty minutes of Chopin played by Vladimir Ashkenazy. I love it.

One evening, soon after the birthday, I put the Chopin on as I was preparing supper. The most unexpected feeling came over me: a wave of sorrow, of lonesomeness, of missing Daddy. I was a little girl again, listening to Chopin with Daddy, me dancing all about. I was four when the dancing lessons began, and he was very indulgent of my new skill. Often he would put "Les Sylphides" on for me at bedtime, loud enough so I could listen as I fell asleep. And so I fell asleep in perfect step with the beautiful dancers on the album cover, and I was wearing white tulle.

On rainy Saturdays I'd sit on his lap and insist on learning the names of all the members of the orchestra while we listened to Mozart, Bach, or Puccini. I thought Michelle Auclaire, first violinist with the Philharmonia, was prettiest. I thought they all lived inside the hifi, the whole orchestra. Very little people.

On fine afternoons, when the light was just right, I would sit on the window box in his bedroom as he sat before his easel and painted. I mixed paints on his palette—burnt sienna, indigo, vermilion. "Who gets to name the colors?" I wanted to know. "I'd like that job." And we would name colors, fantastic, important names. He said he didn't paint well, that it was the doing that was important. While he would never make it as a painter, he thought the better idea was for Uncle Frank and him to write and illustrate *The Baboon Stories*, so we children would have them. It was hard to imagine the book being as entertaining as Daddy and Uncle Frank acting out the stories. We knew they were being made up as they went along, but we could ask for reruns because they always remembered. For adults, they did impromptu Shakespeare, with hats for costumes.

I hadn't visited these memories for many years. All I knew was I was missing him with a painful fervor. It had been more than thirty years. I was too young to lose him, and he was too young to die. And now Chopin. And I remember.

There I stood, facing the window, tears streaming down my cheeks, but quiet. I faced the window, I think hoping the cherry tree, ripe with fruit, would distract me from these sad thoughts. It was suppertime. I did not want to be dripping with the tears, for I could never explain. I knew if I had to explain it would only be worse.

Michael set the table on the porch. A fresh tablecloth, flowers, and such a perfect summer evening. Sweet air, brimming with the perfume of July. We said grace. I kept my head focussed on my plate. I could do this. The music wafted out from the living room. Fortunately Gethin and Eric were heading off to town right after supper, so they couldn't linger. I looked up at Michael as we cleared things away, and I saw that he knew that it was not the time for me to speak, and he did not ask. How grateful I was for that kind space.

I wanted my Daddy back. Dr. Joseph Anthony Gallant—my Daddy. More intensely than I can ever remember wanting him back. But why now? So late? I needed to tell him things, ask him things. He would know. And there are grandchildren, all grown up. I wanted them to know him. Stories about this wonderful, extraordinary man who was their grandfather could never be enough. It hurt me all of a sudden that they could never feel his love that felt like circles of peace all around. They would never know that crooked grin and the twinkle that erupted because the joke was so dry only he got it. He was full of reason when I was not. There was the day I poured out all my cares, somewhat cross at the world for troubling me in such and such a way: "Why me?" He looked at me with the soft, azure eyes and only said, "Why not you?"

How often have I remembered that since this MS affair. Why not me, indeed? He would understand about the MS. Encourage me, applaud my spirit-victory. He would be aching for me, I know—me, his Daddy's Girl—but still there would be the joy. The deep in-the-center-of-you joy. He would never have said, when I confessed about the MS, "Why is my life so full of sorrow?" like Mother did. He would have said, "If anybody can triumph over this, it's you. I'm on your team." Because he knew there is nothing to fear.

There are moments that defined Daddy for me. I came home one day, and there he was in the garage wrecking a small table. Scratching the top, and this after he had already broken one of its legs. My sensible, reasonable, intelligent father.

"What are you doing?" I was stunned.

"Oh, oh. You see I have a patient. She can't pay me. I told her husband, who is a woodworker, that I had a piece of furniture that needed repairs—got damaged—and that I'd be most grateful if he could fix it and that would be payment enough. I couldn't find anything, so I am getting this table ready to be repaired."

Of course. Not breaking it, but getting it ready for repairs. It was me who answered the door a couple weeks later when the table was returned in perfect condition. "Tell Dr. Gallant thank you. My wife is improving all the time." His eyes were bright, and he was proud of his work.

Sometimes there was fresh mackerel or trout, or wild strawberries or blueberries that came to the door and always the same—"Tell the doctor 'thank you.'" This was a poor country. Daddy's private practice carried an optional $2.00/hour fee. Optional, because he believed you could not get better if you had to worry about the doctor's bill. It was a far cry from the $100/hour he would have been paid if he had accepted the offer from the big psychiatric clinic in New York. And this barely in the 1960s. "But here is where I am needed," he always insisted. He was content. I took note. I haven't forgotten. He dreamt of owning a sailboat. Mother said if he would quit giving his money away he could have one.

A bit late, but now I understand the regime for his walks while convalescing from the chemotherapy and radiation. We'd set out and go a safely prescribed distance when he'd say, "Now home again." About turn. He'd set out at what I thought was far too great a pace for a sick man.

"You should take your time so you don't wear out."

"I can't. Only a bit of leg left. I have to hurry or I'll be out of strength before we get home."

Now I know about measuring the distance against the strength in the legs, the time in my legs. Whew! Do I know!

That summer, he'd come with me to the lake most evenings when I got home from work. There was a bench out on the dock and he'd sit there while I dove off, over and over again, and swam back and forth in front of the dock so we could talk or laugh.

It was the way we spent our last summer. He was very thin, but he was so dear. He smiled a lot at me.

All the While

Where are steps before the dawn?
Sheltered in a dream,
surrendered in one waking breath . . .
Inhaled, exhaled, lost. Gone.

Can I hold on one more day?
Perhaps, another few.
Measured animation
my quest, desire, prayer.

A dream of stepping miles:
place to place, on heel and toe.
More brittle than a wish
harder, wincing, all the while.

I might not mind the chair,
were it colored purple,
a sky blue seat, tiny wheels,
someone lovely to push it, there.

8 ❧ AUTUMN MEANS MS CLINIC

utumn is the time for my annual check-up at the MS Clinic. The Clinic made the move to the Victoria General Hospital annex when the old Camp Hill Hospital was finally demolished. I rather like the Clinic's quarters in the MacKenzie Annex. It is unpretentious, and even a little homey. Just fine for me. To find the MS Clinic in that building, I go through the same routine each year, roaming through the maze until finally I find the clinic, with worn-out legs. The signage is not great. It is a good day for one's cane.

Pauline calls me into an examining room and hands me a johnny-shirt, blue or yellow. Always blue or yellow in a gigantic size. There are only pharmaceutical texts to read. I've read them, and they are not very exciting. To pass time, I practice walking in a straight line heel to toe, heel to toe. It is difficult because it requires balance (of which I have only a little sometimes, better others, and none to speak of at others), but it is part of the routine. Jock will ask me to walk the invisible line. Heel to toe and don't look down. Strange little activity. Practicing does not make one bit of difference.

Dr. Murray arrives in a wonderful tie with flowers, usually flowers, very cheerful. We begin. The feather—can I feel it? The pin—when is it sharper? The tuning fork—can I feel the hum? Is it cold—how cold? The feather and the pin questions require astute concentration. The gradations of change are subtle. I wonder if I am imagining the answers. If I imagine I can feel everything, it won't tell Jock anything, except that my imagination is working. The tuning fork is easy—I can't feel the hum at all from hands to several inches above my wrist, nor can I feel its coldness (room temperature to me) till it reaches mid forearm. Imagine my surprise when I finally do feel the cold and the hum!

Next come the strength tests. I still have some strength. I know there is strength in my hands and arms because Michael says I give a good back rub, and I do pull a lot of weeds. Once I lost my right arm, completely, not so long ago, a motor problem of an alarming sort. It's okay at the moment. Then, those balance tests: feet together, and closed eyes. Sway, sway. Think, just think and stand still. Wave, wave, back and forth. The balance problem perplexes me as I cannot deduce the source. I am convinced I am steady, but I could fall right here, right now. Jock promises he won't let me fall. What is off-balance? I have trained myself to walk without the intense concentration needed when the balance problem first appeared. I hardly notice it now until I am in a topple. I have become an observer of walking people.

After these tests, we have a talk. Jock is interested in how I am—different from how I am doing. It is the difference between what the disease is doing to me and what I am doing with the disease. This is an important distinction. I am an optimist. Jock is an optimist. This is our common ground. This strange, eccentric challenge is definitely not the one I would have chosen, but here it is, so I might as well do something with it.

Jock tells me I am doing fine. This understanding of fine is not, "MS will vanish and you will be fine," but rather, he tells me that I am fine, because the part that is me is not my MS. My ability to overcome the challenges of MS is flourishing. I am flourishing. He knows where doing fine comes from, and he bothered to find out if I, too, knew about fine. Most days I know. Most, not all. Dr. Vaughan, to whom Jock sent me for another opinion, told me what he saw the disease doing to me, as well as he could deduce, but he did not look to see where I am on the matter . . . how I am in my head about it. He acquainted himself with half the story, and he missed the side that means something to me. (I think he was rushed.) I was left with the brutal half, and he was left with nothing encouraging to say—the "plain, unembroidered facts."

I took Dr. Vaughan's news with me, although I knew a letter preceded me, as is usual with a consult. Jock did not deny or reinforce Dr. Vaughan's position. I noticed how adroitly he did that. I equally adroitly avoided perusing it, which left Dr. Murray not having to say "progressive." Maybe this was important. Once again, he was able to encourage and prop up my rugged side. It's good he can do this. It is why Dr. Vaughan and I would never have seen eye-to-eye. Not even pretending would make such a relationship compatible.

My condition, it seemed to me in the beginning, was one of the more straightforward cases of MS. There was nothing really remarkable or out-of-the-ordinary about my MS. In the standard presenting way, my MS moved from benign relapse-remitting, to relapse-remitting, to secondary progressive.

"Benign relapse-remitting" meant experiencing exacerbations followed by complete recovery. An exacerbation could present as a spinal cord attack with sensory symptoms such as numbness, loss of position sense, tingling, tight-band feelings, to name a few; or with motor symptoms such as weakness, heavy limbs, loss of dexterity; spasticity (rigidity or stiffness), difficulty walking, bladder hesitancy, constipation, sexual dysfunction; as a brain stem-cerebellar attack with eye movement abnormalities, balance and coordination problems (ataxia), speech disorders, or facial nerve abnormalities, or other symptoms such as swallowing difficulties and emotional lability (a tendency to become sad or happy too easily); as an optic nerve attack which means optic neuritis; or as cerebral attacks—which is rare, with only a three percent incidence, during which symptoms come on like a stroke. Fatigue is considered on its own, since it cannot be attributed to any particular place in the nervous system. It is by far the most misunderstood, debilitating, frustrating symptom of MS, and the most deceptive, as one can look great but feel exhausted.

At this juncture in my journey I said, "I feel rotten for a while, then I am completely well again. This is not so bad. I can do this."

Next phase: "Relapse-remitting." The next change was that symptoms, which appeared during an exacerbation, did not entirely disappear, and over time collected, permanently staying with me. Now that I think of it, this period proved to be the most interesting, to me, at least. According to the literature (*Multiple Sclerosis: Updated Edition*, by Louis J. Rosner and Shelly Ross), "Most attacks will have the features of only one of these patterns—the spinal cord attack, the brain stem-cerebellar attack, the optic nerve attack, or the cerebellar attack. No one develops all these symptoms; most people will have only six or seven symptoms throughout the course of the disease." Six or seven symptoms—well! News to me. I had endured exacerbations during which I experienced a cross-section of symptoms from several sorts of attacks, and, all at once. I certainly had experienced more than six or seven symptoms and decided to make a list. My list included:

Numbness, unpleasant feelings, Lhermitte's sign (an electrical sensation down the back to the arms or legs when the head is bent forward), skin sensations, loss of position sense, numbness in hands and feet, clumsiness, hot and burning feelings, tight band on the trunk, feelings of swelling, extra padding on the soles of the feet, vibrations for no apparent reason, weakness, heavy limbs, loss of dexterity, illegible handwriting, spasticity (as rigidity or stiffness), inability to walk quickly, difficulty using stairs, bladder hesitancy, constipation, double vision, blurred vision, ataxia (balance and coordination problems), sway-tilt-weave-veer or stagger when walking, fine motor skill problems, slurred speech, facial numbness, myokymia (involuntary flickering of facial muscles), trigeminal neuralgia (sharp jabs of electric lightning pain on the face), swallowing difficulty, emotional lability, and, last but not least, the ever-present fatigue. That adds up to thirty-two, and I'm sure I missed some. The only thing that was not hampered with was my sex life, and I cannot imagine how I escaped the commonly experienced symptom of sexual dysfunction.

The next phase, "secondary progressive," moved in. Imperceptibly, I realized that I no longer was having exacerbations. Because of the dramatic nature of my "events," I was glad to be rid of them. What I experienced instead was a constant state of unwellness, of never feeling quite right. It wasn't long before I decided this was easier in some respects. It was predictable, to a certain degree, and manageable. And it did not send me to the Treehouse for weeks and weeks on end. All I had to do was figure out how to carry on while feeling mostly uncomfortable, somewhat miserable, all the time. No relief, but there would be no more events. Once again I said, "This is not so bad. I can do this."

Naturally, I always had questions for Jock, usually much the same. I was interested in the prognosis. Jock told me that my symptoms were primarily sensory, rather than motor (but not the arm). Such symptoms should not seriously handicap me. I would not end up in a wheelchair. Motor symptoms are most troublesome. Can this be true? Will the situation change? So, there is an important distinction between progressive motor and progressive sensory, and I felt this should not be disregarded. It is the ground where stout hearts and hope are intertwined.

I wanted to know if I should be careful, employ some caution. Jock believes in living with gusto. And why not, he assured me I cannot really do anything to hurt myself—what is going to happen is going to happen, no matter what I did or didn't do. He told me about some of his patients who work full-time and travel all over the world—such remarkable people—and how boldly they carry on. I felt small and unadventuresome by comparison. Why couldn't I do that? I wanted to do that . . . and yet . . . I was content in a deep, quiet way.

It took several years before I believed it is only a tenuous connection between what I do and what happens next. Who wants to live in a box of cotton batting anyway?

"So it is all right to continue with my go-till-I-drop routine?"

"Absolutely."

That is one of the many blessings of being home. One couldn't execute this practice in the conventional work-world. Drop (in the garden, on the floor, in the barn, beside the river). Refuel. Work. Drop. I can't imagine what it would look like to a stranger. The family is used to it. Many's the time I have crawled up the steps and into the house. I like to work outdoors. Particularly, there are gardening jobs that are too excellent to leave unfinished, and when working contentedly on hands and knees one might not notice the wear and tear, but try to stand up and . . . whoa! It takes five minutes to exhaust my legs in the garden, thus the appeal of working long-term on ground-level assignments. Earth breaking? Red earth breaking.

There is a downside to this being home, which we share with any family that has experienced the abrupt disappearance of a second income due to chronic illness. I used to imagine I should get a job to help out. I'd think this thought when I was feeling well—typically between 4 and 7 A.M.! Feeling good and ready to get a job! Surprise, not for long. I have come to my senses. The energy I have, I save for my family. I cannot do both. If I had worked all the while the children were little, I would have a nice, fat pension, but I did not do that; instead I stayed home with them. The heart has its own reasons.

I have never been to the clinic when I was crawling or encased in steel or mumbling or anything horrible like that. I would be too tired to go to the clinic then anyway, and would stay home. I forget all these unkind things and so, in the autumn, am disposed to view MS as very tamed. I am sure my doctor thinks I am just great. It is how I am when I visit the clinic, so what else should he believe? At other times, MS rears its most obnoxious side. There is the inevitable exacerbation, very nasty, indeed, then one recovers—in the beginning very well, like a miracle, then later on with much less triumph, MS leaving behind its calling cards of permanent damage.

There is great logic to The Annual Check-Up. It provides essential history for the doctor's ongoing medical assessment—how the disease is progressing, what interventions might be necessary, now that there are some. At last the benefit of the beta-interferon family of drugs (Beta-Seron, Rebif, Avonex), together with Copaxone (glatiramir acetate) offer real hope for reducing the severity and frequency of exacerbations. It is always interesting to hear from Jock what is on the scientific tableau. Also, one likes to clarify the gap between the latest hearsay alternative (sometimes bizarre) treatment, and the advances in medical research. I am convinced Something Big is not far away, and I think it must be in the area of myelin repair. If that can be achieved, we will see people with MS actually improving, for the effects of the disease will be lessened as myelin is repaired. It will be such a moment. Will it be too late for me?

This is a very dynamic disease, which changes in unexpected ways, but yet is predictable to the doctor within certain parameters, if a good watch is kept. I am a very different patient now than the first time I saw Jock. Back then, my MS seemed a straightforward thing involving patience on occasion, and a management plan. The rest of the time, it could be forgotten, because it was invisible. Much has changed. Now each day is a struggle. There's no forgetting about it anymore. I would prefer none of these changes had come to pass, but they have, and they have forever. I know there will be more changes for me, and I won't like these either. The bewildering thing is, I have no way of knowing what will befall me next. It is a mystery. This great unknown is arduous. But I am still walking a little.

I missed one autumn's check-up. Not quite sure how that happened, sort of slipped through the cracks. I thought it was of no consequence since I was holding my own. After eighteen months had gone by I began to wonder what sort of recall I would marshal when faced with reviewing two years' activity. Then I realized I cannot play doctor to myself, especially since the the second year turned out to be one of high MS tumult, and I was not feeling so capable after all at Case Management. That was worthwhile learning.

The annual check-up is important to me. I see my doctor, the optimist, and he assures me that no matter how odd change seems, the picture is not bleak. I'm not sure how he does that—makes one a believer. Surely it is an innate character trait. I sat in the waiting room at the physiotherapist's one day when a woman arrived, took the chair beside me. She walked like I did, and had a cane. A beautiful cane. She told me it was from Mexico and, yes, she, too, had MS. Of course, we fell into instant conversation. She had just come from seeing her doctor. She seemed rattled. She said, "I never know what to say. I feel like I am taking up his precious time. I get all mixed up and nervous. Then I leave feeling ridiculous. It is not a good time for me." I hardly knew what to say. I suppose I wanted to say, "Maybe you should find a new doctor," but I didn't want to further discourage her. I felt sad for her unanswered worries. And I was quietly feeling blessed for having such a thoroughly sanguine experience when I go to my doctor.

When I see Jock, he is already enthusiastic about the day. It is a good way to start. It is just the way he is about life. If he was glum, he'd be wearing a dull gray tie. But no, only wonderful, cheerful ties. The whole examination is calm, reassuring, and unhurried. I have never been made to feel anything I have to ask is silly, anything I worry about is inconsequential, anything I hope for is impossible. Jock is even more optimistic than I am, so I assimilate some of his optimism, and take it home with me. He has lots to go around. He makes me feel capable of enduring the next chapter, and with some humor. One cannot see Jock and be downhearted. And if you are downhearted, you'd best go see him.

I believe him when he says I shall be fine. I launch into another year. And when I tell him, "Thank you, Jock," I mean it. I really mean it.

The Quilt

Since the middle of May my life had been up there, in the Treehouse. Along came June and hay was being made early, for it had been such a glorious spring. The fragrance of both lilacs and new-mown hay wafted in the bedroom windows. There are five of them, the windows. One could sit in bed and look out to the field where the big round bales were being thrust out of the baler. Such a generous crop, so much hay, in spite of all the talk of scanty rain affecting the yields. But cover a left eye and half of the bales disappeared!

Double vision. To combat the annoyance of seeing two of everything, I sported fashion glasses of a homemade sort—one empty lens and one padded lens. Not only was there this seeing double problem, but the left eye would not blink and would not close, even to sleep, which is why padded glasses worked better than a patch.

It shall be remembered as the MS Cyclops Event. They refer to an exacerbation as an event, as though it might be ranked with other social functions one would not want to miss.

One fine day the family decided a picnic was in order and so supper arrived in the Treehouse. It was very delicious and, strangely, my only vivid memory of that event. There were smiling faces of my beloveds, a tablecloth on the floor with the picnic made and set out by Cecily's Shaun, and an evening light shining all golden as it made its way down in the western sky, bathing the room in softness. Much laughter and teasing. How fragrant the air, and how sweet the feel of their care. All the other memories are fuzzy around the edges.

It was the eye and the hand that wore patience thin. A hand that finds a fork of supper a challenge is no help with a needle and thread. A wedding quilt was under production for our eldest son and daughter-in-law-to-be. When the eyes and hands went on leave there were seven squares and a border left to quilt, plus the binding to apply. Time was running out. It seemed the brave but slow assignment of "waiting out" an exacerbation was not going to work this time. One was willing to endure the loss of legs, the tight body case, and most anything else, but, for glory's sake—the quilting gear—please!

Could six weeks be time enough to finish the quilt? This mother of the groom worried not. Finally, the doctor was called to initiate mitigating measures. One takes such measures when chance demands it. Home Care moved into gear and duly three very large doses of intravenous Solu-Medrol were administered in the hopes this would jumpstart our patient, *moi*, out of the exacerbation. There are risks. It is not pleasant, comfortable, or instantaneous, but it does move things along. So came feelings of uneasiness and, at night, strange dreams of able needle-threaders and tiny, tiny quilting needles which made perfect stitches of the sort the Tailor of Gloucester would do.

At last, with three weeks remaining before the departure for Toronto and all the wedding events, things improved, and the window of opportunity was seized. Quilting time was mapped day by day. When the mother and the father of the groom arrived, it was such a moment. Mother gave them their wedding quilt, realizing she had just saved herself from breaking her heart.

Oh, Magnificent Splendor, I can endure much on your behalf, I can forgive you many things, but you should not break my heart.

The Diary

"M ist in the hollow, fine day to follow." That's what they say. I always wondered exactly who "they" are. Must be the meteorologists. In this case they are right. There was a gentle mist in the hollow earlier, then it shaped into a wonderful day. This is a choice place to be—here at the desk, window that looks across the garden and the three-cornered field down to the river. This is the mellow part of September. I went to see Dr. Vaughan on a day like this. I know that because of the notes in my diary.

The winter before the appointment with Dr. Vaughan had been a particularly cantankerous one. There were some pretty weird symptoms; some I never experienced again, some stayed, and have never left.

January 28: Less than a week ago my right side became weak, heavy, and dragged, losing all strength. My knees felt unstable. Now I am doing the whoopsie shuffle. I could not stretch or wiggle the toes on my right foot up, though down was possible with great concentration. My left leg became hot. There has been a pain centered at my waist, between my spine and right side, for several weeks. Sometimes it moves in a line (about the width of a tennis ball), up then back down, going as far as my shoulder. Sometimes it is hardly noticeable, though the point-source spot on my waist is tender to the touch.

February 22: For the first time in two weeks, on February 3, my toes wiggled up and down, and I could lift my leg! The tight band appeared, high on my ribcage. It moved just below my waist by the 5th, then returned to my upper midriff on the 8th. I was quite tottery. Falling asleep was a long trial. Michael falls asleep in about six seconds. No exaggeration.

It would be interesting to wait this out to see what happens, to see if there is much difference in the length of time it takes to recover without Solu-Medrol as with it, although this could be a futile exercise, as every session is quite different, and one never can be certain Solu-Medrol will work. This exacerbation, I can walk (with difficulty), I can see, and I can talk.

Things carried on much the same through mid-February with walking being more or less difficult depending on the day, and the tight band being sometimes so tight that I imagined there were broken ribs, and breathing is sometimes difficult because of this. The band extends from my upper ribcage to pelvic bones. Sleep, however, is much improved.

February 25: Walking with great difficulty. My right side has lost all strength so that I cannot write or eat with my right hand, or even brush my teeth without using two hands to hold the toothbrush. Never having been very ambidextrous, I am getting practice now. I use the keyboard with my left hand and one finger on my right hand. The tight band is uncomfortable day and night. But I can see, and I can speak. Blessedly. The cardboard on the bottom of my feet is very annoying. If I am in such rotten shape now, perhaps I will be pretty good by April or May. Well, except for cardiovascular fitness being a thing of the past. But, if well by May, I will be able to be in the garden and maybe even good for the summer. That would be great, after the last two nasty summers!

The occupational therapist for this area came on Monday to do a home assessment. She didn't have anything to add. I didn't expect anything new, but she is right about getting the bar in the shower.

There is a question that haunts me. Jock says there is nothing one can do to hurt oneself, that what is going to happen will happen regardless of what one does. But it appears there are things that can cause a break in the blood-brain barrier, an event necessary for an exacerbation to occur. Can there not be events in one's life that therefore do influence the progress of the disease? What are they? This confuses me greatly. Make a note to ask Jock.

March 31: After weeks of it being closed, on March 14, my right hand opens! It was hard work but it opened. The improvement continued during the week till it opened normally by the 22nd. The pins and needles and sandpaper sensation remain. Somewhat steadier, I get around with a cane when out of the house. I went to church on Palm Sunday for the first time in a month. I still do not drive. I am not sure if I should rest or build up stamina by forging ahead . . . think I'll forge onward. This is slow, but I am not polluted with Solu-Medrol. The tight band and tight-bottomed feet persist.

April 14: There was improvement in early April, however small, and I resumed choir practice with Michael. Stamina is still at a premium. I am driving again, and I will go to town, if it is truly necessary, but make a careful calculation of the distance from the car to my destination before I disembark. One day, parked just near the TD Bank foyer (lucky spot) that enclosed the banking machine, I counted, as best as possible, the steps to the parking meter and then to the banking machine. In all about 20 to 25 steps, one way. Barely made it. On days like these I am grateful for a handicapped parking card. I don't like to use it otherwise as I expect there will always be somebody who needs it more. Usually I can get where I am going and start out feeling okay, but the return trip is difficult. There are not enough places for people like me to sit and restore ourselves. Truly, I do not much like going to town. Wears me out. Nowhere to drop when I want.

April 16: Worked in the garden. It was such a glorious day. Felt hopeful.

April 30: Gethin got home. My dream is to be able to walk without thinking about it. It interests me, when in town, to watch people walking by, and I try to imagine how many of them are walking successfully only because they are thinking about it. I sit in the car and watch people's feet go by. The world's shoes are in a dreadful state. I can tell when somebody is concentrating on their steps. I know that concentration. They look like I do. One foot, other foot, how much farther? That's the drill.

May 20: The tight band released on May 15, and only a taped-up feeling remained on the soles of my feet. But the fatigue! Always the fatigue! The poor weather has been a blessing, for it is definitely not gardening weather. When the long weekend came I gardened by dint of a work, rest, work, rest scheme. Five busy days in the garden, then a three-day collapse! I went to the Magic Glade for the first time since December, with my woods stick for support. I told the kids if I was not home in two hours to come looking for me. Made it there and back in exactly in two hours. It is really a half-hour walk.

Will the numbness in my hands and feet likely go away?

August 1: We had an Edward Family Reunion in July. There were twenty-five of us here for a week of catching up, fun, hilarity, competition (croquet and baseball tournaments, treasure hunt, magic show, golf, windsurfing, beach fests, team cooking, and a daily press conference to report on sporting events). I survived it well. That's because everyone helped with everything. We had fun! I did it! No. I didn't do it. The whole family did it, and I was simply one of twenty-five, crazily swept along in its wake. The soreness was from laughter. The good kind of sore. The kids said it was awesome. They are right.

September 30: Early August arrived, and my back grew very tight. Different from the tight band. The tightness stretched across my entire back in a band from my waist and up about six inches. It felt very sore, as though I have put my back out, and it is just healing. Also, it felt as if I was being pushed forward, which had an impact on my balance. At the same time, there was a feeling of heavy bearing down in my lower abdomen. These opposing forces of being pushed down and forward made walking a very thoughtful process. Tricky without a cane. Impossible without a cane, for now. Once in a while there is a day when I feel pretty good. Most of the time it is struggle with the walking and the fatigue. Bother! I liked a brisk step, and I had the importance of good posture drilled into me by my dance instructors.

It's the end of September and these symptoms persist with little change. A rare head cold magnified all the symptoms for a few days till the cold calmed down. I am in one pathetic state of fitness. It's pretty bad when muscles are the stuff of dreams.

Today was my appointment with Dr. Vaughan. It is somewhat novel and a blessing for the Island to have a neurologist for a change, a real neurologist. Everybody thinks highly of the young Dr. Vaughan. We hear only good things about him. A student of Jock's, Dr. Vaughan shows great promise. People say he is thorough, precise, compassionate. It was Jock's request for a second opinion.

I was called into his office and found Dr. Vaughan poring over some papers, trying to get a sandwich and a cup of coffee down, a fringe of Beatle-like bangs falling straight across his forehead. It made him look all the younger. I understood he was a very busy man, and I would have gladly waited while he had a bit of lunch. "No, no, come in," he said. So I did.

We had to start at the beginning so he could create a medical profile for me. With some cryptic notes to help me remember things chronologically, especially things one would rather forget, we began. The diary was helpful, beginning as it did with November 1990. He asked so many questions, which I answered, answered, and answered. All the while he wrote on a page of paper that was quickly filling up. He squashed as much as he could on that one page, and when he got to the bottom he turned it around and began making use of the margins. Somebody give the doctor paper!

When every possible space had been written on, we went into the examining room. The usual neurological exam I had grown accustomed to followed. Pins. Feathers. Was this sharp, or could I feel this? Balance tests. He sat down on the footstool. I was sitting on the examining table, an odd reversal of psychological advantage. He told me the diagnosis had changed from benign to progressive. (Go away, I don't want to listen!) He was looking very sad while he spoke, so I told him he must not worry, as I was coming to that conclusion on my own. This was stretching it a bit because I was certainly not wanting to believe this conclusion, but he was so young and so earnest. I asked what he thought about beta interferon. He said it has very little effect on the actual MS condition, that its success lies in improving an MRI reading, but it does little for the patient. Whew. This doctor was not encouraging at all. I offered the insight that Jock's view was a far more optimistic one. He said that was because "Jock is an entirely optimistic person," while he was "optimistic but realistic." Being an optimist myself, I concluded there was not much chance of this becoming an exemplary doctor-patient affiliation.

I drove home knowing everything must now change, in my head. I would have to make the change from thinking of the disease as an infernal pest that would not permanently handicap me, to a disease that had the potential of causing any manner of trouble and unknown disability.

October 1: Michael and I woke early and talked this morning for a long time. I feel this disease gravely today, unlike in the past. What if I cannot get to the woods?"

Clear Lens

Rain came down reminding
me of you and me when we
were young and unaware how
some things change and
some things stay the same,
though time and age stand between
old bright-eyed love of wondering why and
new cherished love of believing how—
then looking through a clear lens,
seeing the best never changes
but simply is.

9 🌿 BLOSSOM COUNT

Today, I know it is too far to get to the woods on my own steam. But on Sunday we took a picnic to Basin Head. As is usual for us when settling at the beach, we walked till we were far from the madding crowd. That means me! I walked in the sand, all that way. Inconceivable two months ago. Then a wonderful swim. Supper and the return walk. Amazing. I was wiped for three days following, but it was worth the triumph! And since I cannot go hiking, I believe it is a good day for a blossom count. The blossom count is a stand-in for being able to tear about as I please, but practical as I'll need help remembering all this next spring when I refine the plan. There needs to be more place for flowers, as all the perennials need dividing. It is a big mess of too much stuff. I can't keep up.

Changing things is a good plan. We don't need so much of a vegetable garden with the kids off on their own, more and more. So it will be just the two of us. It feels very different, after years of being a formidable team. Michael and I must contrive ways to make the operation here more manageable, considering my limitations, and his limited availability in May and June because of so much going on at school. All of a sudden this summer we realized how our workforce had shrunk. Certainly we must reduce the strawberry patch by three-quarters. Eric proposes we change the vegetable garden to raised beds that will reduce our labor. We surely don't need all that food anymore.

There was more I wanted to do this spring, but I was feeling so rotten, it was not possible. Yet, there were a few new blue additions: cornflower, bluebells of Scotland, and a gift of scabiosa from Lois MacLaren, who is a wonderful gardener. She has a greenhouse. Lois sits in front of me at choir, in the alto row. In the spring she arrives at choir practice with plants from her greenhouse to go to their new home in my garden. This is always great excitement to me. Lois is in her eighties, though nobody believes this because she looks considerably younger. She has a young heart. Anyway, I had never seen scabiosa before. Its blossom is a most exquisite, almost translucent pale blue with a pink center—gorgeous. My Edward sisters—Allyson,

Molly, and Peggy—gave me two day lilies for my birthday: Respighi, a rich burgundy with yellow center, and Enchanted Butterfly, which will be a surprise. Since I had Respighi in the garden I figured I should familiarize myself with Ottorino Respighi's music and so I borrowed *La Boutique Fantastique* (twelve movements) from the library. Very robust and rambunctious like the day lily named after it. I started some petunia from seed: prism sunrise (pale yellow) and chiffon morn (pale pink with yellow centers) and am proud of these, as they are doing wonderfully.

The blossom count still pleases me, in spite of the raucous and somewhat untended condition of the garden. Along with the new things, there are black-eyed Susan, purple coneflower, phlox (pink-white, fuchsia, white), ageratum, delphinium (white, blue), campanula, golden yarrow, lettuce poppy (pink), spiderwort, borage, feverfew, viola, tiger lily, Asiatic lily (yellow, pink, white-pink), veronica (speedwell-purple, pink, white), harebell (purple, white, lavender), pansies (every color), Oriental poppy, cinquefoil (yellow, white), Cupid's dart, orange day lily, astilbe, lavender (hardy and English), calendula, nasturtium, bergamot, yellow alyssum, begonia (yellow, peach, orange, pink), New Guinea impatiens (salmon), trailing lobelia (blue-white), standing lobelia (blue), geranium (red, pink), marigold (yellow), sweet William, roses (pink, fuchsia), and wildflowers in the orchard: wild roses, mallow, St. John's wort, goldenrod, Queen Anne's lace, evening primrose, mallow, common yarrow (white), mullein, and bouncing Bet.

There are other new things in blossom which I, myself, planted, and I have no idea what they are. I have forgotten. I didn't put identifying markers with them. (I forget that I forget.) I wonder how this memory thing works? Mine is not so good anymore. I know that I know, but I cannot pull the file. Eventually, maybe hours later or the next day, I find it. Sometimes not at all. I tried some ginseng since there was an impressive list, ten to be exact, of benefits in taking ginseng. The first one was "restores memory." I took the ginseng every day for a month. I quickly forgot what the other nine were. No more ginseng.

I think I shall get to the woods later today to see the blossoms there, and because it seems to me that after last evening's line squall, which dumped a straight-down good rain on us, there should be chanterelles. It did not harm the grain, which stands at least three feet tall. I have a new recipe for wild rice and mushroom soup. I think chanterelles would be wonderful in that soup. I'll get Michael to take me on the tractor. I've tried the tractor myself, but it is too much machine. Coming home through the hollow, down the hill is a bit tricky for me because the clutch and brake are stiff, and by then I am worn out. Not safe. I need an old ride-on mower without the deck or a golf cart (doesn't matter how dilapidated), so I can get to the woods on my own. I spoke to the man at Harding Medical Supply, and he advises that a scooter is meant for pavement and would not be safe on rough ground; that a battery-run golf cart is too low-slung; that an old gas-powered golf cart would be safest. That would make me very happy. I would feel independent, and I could putter about the farm much better, as my legs would last longer. It's the walking about that finishes them.

It is important to be able to get to the woods. I started taking Gethin for walks to the woods when he was a month old. And then Cecily joined us and then Eric. It was fun with the three of them. A good day was made better, and a bad day could be turned around with a rousing game of hide-and-seek in the Magic Glade. I used to go there to think and restore myself. I miss it so. When I needed a break I would "run away" (mothers of small children sometimes need to run away) to the woods. I'd find a mossy spot and lie in it, looking up at the sky through the forest canopy. It didn't take long before I returned home thinking everything was just grand.

Independence. A beat-up old golf cart. That's all.

Harley and Mr. K

One day, Harley the golf cart appeared in my life as an answer to a dream, and everything changed, for a while. Then he grew old and undependable.

"We are stuck in the woods again, Harley. Thee and me. You won't move, will you! Now what? Nobody is at home and, besides, I didn't leave a note. If someone comes home soon and sees we are both gone, then, presumably, after an hour or so, they'll figure out we are stuck. I am no mechanic, but the problem is your ignition. That means wires. I wonder if fiddling with wires causes electrocution? I've never much cared how machines work till now, and I only want to cause you to go again, and that is all. Oh, Harley! Really. Your ignition and my legs equal a frightful combination."

Three cooling breaths . . . phwoo, phwoo, phwoo. I'll put you in neutral and let you roll backwards down this slope. Gravity. Thank goodness. Now think.

Here we sit, just beyond the Daddy Pine. It is so beautiful in the woods. I need to be here in this green fragrance. There's the tree where the barred owl looked menacingly at me as I ran by that day. I was startled. He was so huge, and his eyes, in that turning head, followed me, glowering, making me feel like an intruder in my own forest.

"It's okay," I say, "just passing through and no danger to you." He lets a dog-like howl, spreads his massive wings, and lifts off his perch, answering a corresponding call a short distance away. I duck, though he is high above me, then I catch my breath and continue on my way.

If I ran from the yard, down the front lane, back to the yard and down the back lane to the Hollow, up the far side by the Logging Yard, went in Middle Road to the Magic Glade, along River Road to the Cove and back to the Hollow then home again and repeated this three times, I'd have run four miles, an alternative to the smooth, relaxed route along the Rosebery Road. I thought it strengthening for ankles to run on the forest floor, mossy but uneven. And there was always cool air in the Hollow, sweet relief on a hot day. Once I nearly stepped on a young skunk. We were both startled and took off in opposite directions.

And now I am here and cannot even walk home.

I wonder how long it would take to walk home? I could walk two hundred steps, then stop and rest. There's a book in Harley's dash, so I could read during the breaks. No. Too slow. It would take hours. I would rather take my chance with the wires.

"This looks fairly simple, Harley, just a couple of wires. That one must connect to something. Try that. Hmm . . . Varoom . . . We're off! Just keep going, Harley, and don't stop till we're home."

There was some discussion following this event, which I have to confess repeated itself several times, as I insisted I needed to get to the woods, and so I went. Harley was no longer a faithful companion. He was showing his age and could no longer be depended upon. Leon and Joshua Nicholson, Harley's mechanics, who worked with endless patience and the curiosity to fuss, had pushed the absolute limits in repairing Harley's decrepit parts. There was one last chance for Harley. Michael and I set off for Vesey's in York to visit the shop where Harley-Davidson parts were stocked. But none, it turned out, for old gas golf carts that had not been manufactured for twenty years. "There are no more parts. Putting money in that old thing would be like burying it in a hole in the ground." Sounded a bit harsh: "that old thing."

That was the day we test-drove the Kawasaki. First, I drove. It seemed perfect to me. Then it was Michael's turn, and he went too fast (I thought), going up and down over rough ground. He wanted to know how it would maneuver in the woods. He was very satisfied. It had all-terrain tires, more power than I would ever need, a frank sturdiness, excellent stability, and easy handling. Kawasaki calls it "The Mule." I did not care for the name, as it implied a stubborn, single-minded, I'll-do-what-I-like nature, and I was in the mood to be The Boss. I was sure I would never call it "The Mule." There is a bench seat, easy to get into with places for two (a grandchild, a friend), and a dump box behind. Seat belts, a rollbar, and even headlights. No horn. But I don't need a horn.

That demo model was red. I could order green, which caught my attention for a moment, but our tractor, trailer, and tiller are all red. This would be part of a brigade; one of a team. And I would be easy to spot in the woods. Besides, tomatoes are red, as are poppies and the dawn. Red is just fine. For me, a singular aid, not in the way of even the fanciest electric scooters, which couldn't take me anywhere I need to go. I want to go everywhere on the farm. One day, some months later, the Kawasaki was delivered to me. I call him "Mr. K" or, affectionately, just "K." He has a place in the barn alongside the rest.

There is a compartment in Mr. K's dash where I keep sunscreen, a walkie-talkie with a radius of two miles, scissors for clipping chanterelles or for picking bouquets, and an old pair of sunglasses. In the shelf in the dash, I keep my *Guide to the Wildflowers of PEI*, a bottle of water, an apple, and some bugstuff. In the box behind, my gardening equipment, including a stack of three rubber baskets (green, red, blue) that are endlessly versatile, as one basket can be scrunched to fit perfectly on the floor of the passenger's side. I pitch compost or whatever I need right into the basket, drive back to the garden, and roll it off with hardly any lifting. Before these, I had to ask and ask and ask for help to accomplish things I wanted to do myself. There is a reed basket for small tools, gardening gloves, seeds and such. The larger tools (hoe, spade, rake) plus a watering can fit in the box, too, and, tucked along one side, my English chestnut cane for walking in the woods if there is no hand for me to hold. Or there might be bamboo sticks and poles, stakes, a rubber-headed mallet, binder twine, bone-meal, buckwheat, a bucket of stones. You never know. Or the camera, a notebook, binoculars, a picnic basket, and a blanket.

Michael keeps a trail mowed around the Three-Cornered Field. It makes an excellent drive along the river and is perfect for watching ducks, which make a home on the millpond with their broods. It is also perfect for seeing trout jumping or eagles heading out in the morning or home at the end of the day on their fly-path up the river to their nests. Michael mows the woods trail as far as the Bush-hog can go. He is amused that I always stop at the Hollow when coming out of the woods from the River Road and look both ways before heading up the hill and home. He asks, grinning,

"Any traffic today?" Who do I imagine I will run into? A snow-shoe hare? A skunk? A fox? But I always stop and look both ways.

I had that sad day—that maybe I won't be able to get to the woods, one day—and I was thinking about grandchildren. He promised me I would always be able to get to the woods; that a way would be found—no matter what. I am more thrilled with Mr. K than an eighteen-year-old boy with the keys to a Corvette. I love Mr. K.

Clean-up

I have been enjoying myself doing all those preparing-for-Christmas things I could not have dreamed of doing last year. I have made gifts for all the kids. A futon-sized quilt for Gethin, a memory box of our trip to New York for Cecily, a big polar fleece robe for Eric. Gathered small treasures for stockings. Hunted down books and music. There is much baking stored away to mellow.

The weather has been decidedly wintry and never so at such an early date. We received our first snowstorm the last week in November, then another the following week, and it has stayed. This took us by surprise, and after a fall of inclement Saturdays we have not done the garden clean-up. Something messy will face us in spring.

There were many times I thought of getting a start at it, but that is all it ever is with work like that, a start. There is something about that kind of labor that finishes off my legs in a matter of minutes. All I need do is haul the garden cart out of the barn, filled with tools and the things I need for the job, and head for the garden. By the time I have "set up" at a plot, I feel my legs weakening. I try to simplify as much of a job as I can. So rather than putting the baskets near the crop and filling them, I leave the baskets in the cart and fill them there, knowing I cannot lift a full basket on board.

Not very long ago, this would have barely been a warm-up, and now it is my doing-in. Before, I could have heaved as many baskets as produce filled, cleaned away debris to the compost, tilled the plot, and still have had half a day before me. Now, getting the cart into the barn is a major opus. It is strange to see how there is no strength in me because it isn't that I feel weak, but I guess I shall have to admit I am that decrepit. I don't feel decrepit. In my mind, I don't. I imagine I can do things the same as I always did. Odd to have a head that feels the same as ever but a body that doesn't work. Just plain odd.

Not Me

There is a person living around here with an illness. It is a significant chronic illness with serious symptoms that change life wholly and utterly. A sober and melancholy reality. I watch with some interest. Curiosity. Fascination. Because it is me. My illness. What is illness? The Oxford says it is "unhealthy condition of body, sickness."

I should think it is somebody else with this illness, this multiple sclerosis. I don't get sick and I never have, not anything to speak about. I didn't miss a day of school until a twenty-four-hour flu kept me out of grade five for two days. One day sick and one for good measure.

There were the usual illnesses—mumps, measles, and chicken pox—before I started school. And none of those I recall as much of an event. I believe there were two chicken pox. Mumps not serious. I think measles was the biggest incident. Tom had tonsillitis so they took mine out, too, for good measure, when I was five. It was in the days when everybody was doomed to have their tonsils out, so might as well do it before school started. There must have been some phobia about kids missing school. Otherwise, except for that one little flu, perfect attendance until high school. During Christmas holidays, when I was eleven, somebody had the bright idea to straighten out a middling hammertoe by removing the first joint in the toe. It was not successful, since it created a worse problem, but I did not miss even a day of school.

There was a flu one summer when I was twelve, an odd flu. I remember a fever and great dizziness. I could only drink from a flexible straw because I was too woozy to sit up to eat. It took five days out of my summer, then left as quickly as it came. I have a clear picture of me that day, hopping on my bike, all better, flying across the baseball field in my favorite shorts and top. The shorts were purple with narrow white stripes set far apart, and there was a buttonless, short-sleeved jacket that had narrow white, purple, and green stripes set close together, and a white tank top. The outfit was a hand-me-down from Catherine Anne, all the way from Oregon. Odd I should remember these details. And I swallowed a fly. I remember that, too. Pedaling along, laughing with my mouth open. It flew out my nose. It was the day I learned that it was true about the eustachian tube connecting everything. Nothing like field work to prove a scientific fact. Was this The Virus? The one that hid there, latent, waiting for the other factors to play into the emergence of MS? I wonder. Wish they would find the virus.

Once there was food poisoning. Dysentery in Morocco. And a breast infection when Eric was a baby. Some head colds. That's about it. I never had PMS and didn't even know what it was. My period came every fourth Tuesday at 4 P.M., without any bother. I did not miss a basketball practice or game, a dancing lesson or social event. I had a boil once, on my knee and then one on my thigh. I got reading glasses when I went to college. Gethin, Cecily, and Eric were each born seven days early, no keeping me waiting. They arrived without fuss and without any intervention. I found labor highly exciting, knowing the prize on the way, and the births exhilarating and thrilling, with that satisfaction that must only come at the finish line of something big, like a marathon, but this finish, an extraordinary beginning.

When they were just little, my right leg began to be a bad leg. Not all the time, but every so often, it became heavy like lead. I was running regularly, about twenty miles a week, and there were many days it felt as if there was somebody else running with me, behind me, pulling on a band that held my legs back. It could be very hard work running against this opposing force. When it wasn't there, I could go like the wind. This was so much fun I could not help grinning ear to ear as I ran along. I expect that was why I kept it up. The good days were too good not to miss. Bad leg must be related to the pregnancies.

Next my hands played a few tricks on me. A glass would slip without cause. My writing changed. My good writing became messy writing. This, I believed, was very likely because I nearly lost the tip of my baby finger on my right hand, and it was terribly stiff and full of pins and needles for years after having it sewn back on. Surely that was it. Then, all of a sudden, the handwriting improved. Back to normal. Finding a good pen is a chore, but when you find one, it's great. I was sure it was the pen.

These two afflictions—the difficulty running and the difficulty with my hands—would, in the end, signal something was wrong.

Something real and something big. I could not attribute these any more to pregnancy, to cuts and bruises, or to lost pens. And so I knew.

Nobody known to me, in the wider family circle, is known to have had MS. Nobody. MS was some condition that one heard about but did not ever think about. There were wheelchairs and drooping heads. Canes. That could never be me. I'm healthy. I'm a runner. No, not me. So if this isn't me, who is it? Get a grip, girl. It is me. And in a sounder frame of mind, I know it doesn't matter.

There was this very sad day. Michael went running. Cecily went running. Eric went for a row. Gethin mowed. I had no energy and no legs. That was a Saturday. I tried to keep up my nerve. By Sunday afternoon I was feeling pretty sad. I cuddled up in Michael's arms with my tale of woe, and he listened. How I wanted to feel good, even for one hour. Normal. I would go for a walk or a run. One hour a month to feel normal would be all I would need. For one hour I would walk—no, run—without thinking about it and not grow weary. Oh! it would be fine. It will never be fine. This is forever. It is a blessing to have my beloved to remind me how I am cherished, adored, loved without measure. I am me to my husband with or without this MS-ness. Not what I do, but what I am. Isn't a husband a wonderful idea? Best husband. Beloved Michael. Archangel.

Every once in a blue moon this sadness hits me. No doubt it will do so again, but blessedly it is short-lived. As I grow in spirit and in strength, it will not grieve me so. The problem is I still remember what it felt like to be truly strong in my body. I want it back. Being strong in spirit: there's the challenge. It isn't about getting back to the parking space without a cane. It is about knowing I am not part of the cane, but as wonderful a creation as the hand that holds it or the hand that made it, so I can use it when I need it.

Holding Hearts

Several dreams ago
you put my hand in yours
and held it there,
afraid I might be lost
and never found again.
I heard a lost story like
those on the radio.

Several lives ago
I put my heart in yours
and kept it there,
knowing I had been found
never to be lost again.
I wrote a found story like
those with happy endings.

Just the other day
I lost my way,
        reached out
your hand was there
wrapped in my heart.

Acknowledgments

Most earnest thanks to Dr. T. Jock Murray, who saw fodder for a book in the notes I sent for my file. His literary charge to me was compelling, and I was not in a mind to say "no" to Jock. Truly, this book did not begin in the usual way. For inestimable care of my health and for support throughout this journey, thank you, Jock.

Thanks to my brother, Tom Gallant, who worked with me on the original manuscript. I loved listening to him talk about writing. We laughed a lot. I treasure those days.

Thanks to my professors, David Aurandt and Frank Ledwell, who, many years after my sitting in their classes, still teach me. It was their enthusiasm and support for the book that led me to the publisher I needed. I felt like I was handing in an assignment; one should never lose that feeling.

To Anne Chisholm, Harry Baglole, Loran Fevens, Dr. W. J. Hankey, Elizabeth Kromer, Helen Steinberg, and Dr. Elizabeth Townsend: sincere thanks for your assistance and support, and especially to Dr. Barbara Flanagan for many years of exemplary family doctoring to our whole clan.

To my lively parish family of St. Peter's Cathedral—its clergy, people, and particularly the Choir and the vanDames. Bless you. Life wouldn't be nearly as joyful without you.

I longed to have the book in the hands of Laurie Brinklow, whom I consider a most gifted publisher. The circuitous route I took to reach her was worth it. My editor at Acorn Press, Jane Ledwell, has been a gem to work with. Her intelligence, insight, enthusiasm, warmth, and relentless insistence I get it right are deeply appreciated.

Lastly, and most importantly, to my family whom I adore—you are my life, and there is no journey without you. So, to my husband Michael, our children Gethin and Meg, Cecily and Shaun, Eric and Lisa, and to our grandchildren Steven, Ruby, Joseph, Isaac, Crispin, and Samuel. I love you beyond speaking, writing, or thinking.

—Catherine Edward, January 2008

National Multiple Sclerosis Organizations

National Multiple Sclerosis Society
733 Third Avenue, 3rd floor
New York, NY 10017
Toll-free: (800) 344-4867
Web: www.nationalmssociety.org
Includes search engine for local chapters

Multiple Sclerosis Association of America
706 Haddonfield Road
Cherry Hill, NJ 08002
Toll-free: (800)532-7667
Main Telephone: (856) 488-4500
Main Fax: (856) 661-9797
E-mail: webmaster@msassociation.org
Web: http://www.msassociation.org

About the Author

Catherine Edward was born in Saint John, New Brunswick, and grew up in Pendleton, Oregon, and on Canada's Maritime coast. She is a graduate of Collège Notre-Dame d'Acadie and the University of PEI. She worked with the CBC National Radio Network in Toronto and London, UK, made regular appearances on CBC TV's national game show *What Is It?*, worked as a television current-affairs scriptwriter in Charlottetown, PEI, and throughout Peter Gzowski's tenure at CBC Radio's flagship, *Morningside*, she was a frequent panelist. Edward has written for *Atlantic Insight Magazine*, *PEI Profiles*, *Golden Times Magazine*, and *The Anglican Planet*. She was a nationally syndicated columnist for CBC Radio, a production assistant with CBC Radio, and Special Projects Coordinator for the Institute of Island Studies at the University of Prince Edward Island. She is currently a member of the Board of Directors of MS Atlantic and a member of MS Canada's National Caregivers Advisory Group. She is a former Board member of the Sir Andrew Macphail Homestead Foundation, the Eldon Women's Institute, St. Peter's Cathedral Mothers' Union, and is a District Advisor for La Leche League Interntational. She and her husband, Michael, have three married children and six grandchildren. They live in Belfast, Prince Edward Island.

A Note on the Type

The text was set in 11.5 point Adobe Brioso Pro Regular with a leading of 14.5 points space. Designed by Robert Slimbach, Brioso is an energetic type family modeled on formal roman and italic script. In the modern calligrapher's repertoire of lettering styles, roman script is the hand that most closely mirrors the oldstyle types that we commonly use today; it is also among the most challenging styles to master. Named after the Italian word for "lively," words set in Brioso move rhythmically across the page with an energy that is tempered by an ordered structure and lucid form.

The display font is Adobe Brioso Pro Medium Italic. Evoking the look of a finely penned roman and italic script, it retains the immediacy of hand lettering while having the scope and functionality of a contemporary composition family.

Design by Jean Carbain

Printed in the U.S.A.